JUDAI(K)ITSCH

JUDAI(K)ITSCH

tchotchkes, schmattes, and nosherei

by **Jennifer Traig** and **Victoria Traig**   photographs by **Dwight Eschliman**

CHRONICLE BOOKS

SAN FRANCISCO

Library of Congress Cataloging-in-Publication Data:

Traig, Jennifer.
    Judaikitsch : tchotchkes, schmattes, and nosherei / by
Jennifer Traig and Victoria Traig.
        p. cm.
    ISBN 0-8118-3188-4
        1. Jewish crafts—United States. 2. Cookery, Jewish.
3. Kitsch—United States. 4. Popular culture—Religious
aspects—Judaism. 5. Fasts and feasts—Judaism. 6. Jewish
wit and humor. I. Traig, Victoria. II. Title.

BM729.H35 T73 2002
745.5'088296—dc21
                    2001028221

Printed in China

Designed by Benjamin Shaykin
Typeset in New Century Schoolbook, Futura,
Hebrew Graphic One, Shalom, and Monterey
Next year in Jerusalem!

Photo assistants: Darrell Coughlin, Kaija Jones,
Tom Ontiveros
Food stylist: Diane Gselle

Distributed in Canada by
Raincoast Books
9050 Shaughnessy Street
Vancouver, British Columbia V6P 6E5

10 9 8 7 6 5 4 3 2 1

Chronicle Books LLC
85 Second Street
San Francisco, California 94105

www.chroniclebooks.com

For our parents, Alain and Judy.
We hope this brings them naches.

TABLET OF CONTENTS

FUNNY, YOU DON'T *LOOK* JEWISH
a word on icons and a brief history of kitsch

Ever since that unfortunate incident with the golden calf, Judaism has shied away from the plastic arts. Sure, we've got tasteful silver kiddush cups and some nice stained glass, but the religion lacks the fabulous kitschy statuary and icons so many other religions enjoy. We don't have Moses birdbaths in our yards, holographic Miriam keychains, or King David nightlights by our beds. Kitsch requires a system of references, an iconography, and iconographies are almost always unkosher (see golden calf, above). The world is full of doodads, but Jewdads are few.

Judaikitsch: Tchotchkes, Schmattes, and Nosherei aims to fill that void with a campy collection of crafts and cooking ideas. We hope to be your funky, festive Jewish lifestyle guide. And we hope to open your eyes to the Jewish kitsch all around you. Jewish culture *does* have its icons—they're just a little less obvious. They consist of Manischewitz boxes and Mogen David bottles, of Barbra Streisand and Bette Midler, of matzo ball mixes and Jewish mother jokes.

Jewish kitsch has a long and proud history. You've seen it in museums and in your own home: a nineteenth-century

The Classic Bar Mitzvah Troll.
Just what every thirteen-year-old boy wants: a doll.

menagerie menorah, antique souvenirs from the Holy Land, the '50s Maxwell House hagaddah your grandparents used, the Bart Simpson yarmulke you wore at your Bar Mitzvah. They're artifacts of our shared past—sometimes happy, sometimes hard.

And they've been around for a long, long time. The word *tchotchke* is about 500 years old, so we can assume the items it describes have been around even longer. When Eastern European Jews came to America in the late 1880s, they brought their kitschy tchotchkes with them. Not everyone was happy about this. German Jews, who'd been in America a good deal longer, were particularly dismayed by the new immigrants' tacky trappings. These more established Jews spearheaded campaigns to help the new arrivals decorate tastefully, making house calls to preach their mantra of "Simplify, simplify, simplify." But their pleas fell on deaf ears. Instead of jettisoning their kitsch, many immigrants simply added to it, enhancing their collections with the cheap consumer goods readily available in their new homeland. There goes the neighborhood.

Here comes gastrointestinal distress. If the immigrants' taste in decorating made some folks sick, their cooking must have made them even sicker. Oh, we love traditional Jewish food, of course. But only because we grew up eating it. If you're not Jewish, gefilte fish holds little appeal. The first time we brought a non-Jewish friend home for Passover, disaster ensued. "Why are you trying to feed me cat food?" he choked. "Is this really how it's supposed to taste? Is it supposed to be *sweet?*" Yes, it is, but we'll get to that later (see Castaway Carrot Candy, page 80). What our friend failed to realize is that taste is secondary in Jewish cooking. Artistic expression comes first. The energy Jews could have been putting into the plastic arts all these years went into creative cooking instead. In other words, we stopped sculpting calves and started sculpting veal. The majority of our traditional foods are symbolic representations. Hamantaschen are hats or ears; bagels are stirrups; haroset is mortar. In the 1940s and 1950s this practice reached its kitsch height, as Jewish cookbooks encouraged homemakers to play with their food. They were instructed to build salads into menorahs, sandwiches into Maccabean soldiers, blintzes into Tablets of Law. Here was food that didn't just taste bad—it actually was in bad taste.

But who are we to say? We are reluctant to make cultural value judgments, though such judgments are crucial to the history of kitsch. The word *kitsch* comes from the German words *verkitschen* (to cheapen) and *kitschen* (to collect junk). It was originally intended to denote the opposite of *kultur,* or high art. Kultur is highbrow. Kitsch is lowbrow. And then there is camp, which can only be described as arched-brow. Camp is kitsch that's in on the joke. Obviously, then, much of the material in this book falls into that category. But one man's camp is another man's kitsch, is yet another man's kultur.

Yes, even that ridiculous Hanukkah Headband (see page 88)—that's somebody's kultur. Just because it's cute and funny and sometimes irreverent, doesn't mean it's not historically and culturally significant. So we think it's important to emphasize that we really are sincere about the subject. Kitsch records where we've been and where we're going. It's our communal inheritance. You were hoping for the silver? You got the Mah-Jongg Menorah (see page 87) instead. We hope you cherish it.

HOW TO USE THIS BOOK

One of us is strictly observant, and one of us is non-practicing. One of us is a professional artist, and one of us is a casual home-crafter. One of us is a hostess with the mostest, and one of us is a hostess with not so much. We're both firm believers that it's your thing—do what you want to do. We've tried to compile a book that will suit Jews and non-Jews of all artistic aptitudes, kitchen capabilities, and observance levels. If you belong to a chavurah, subscribe to *Tikkun,* or surf tattoojew.com, this is the craft cookbook for you. It's also for you if you're new or non-practicing and are just looking for a fun, easy way to connect to the Jewish tradition.

the crafts Having said all that, we admit that a few of these crafts are a little ambitious. Some require a kiln; others, a pathological neurosis for detail. If you are Jewish you probably have the latter, but are unlikely to own any heavy-duty clay-firing equipment. Fret not. We've got easy alternative how-tos, using normal household supplies, for all the challenging projects. If that still seems too challenging, you can use the projects as idea source material, and adapt them to crafts that are more your speed. But maybe you should push yourself a little, *nu?*

the food The cardinal rule of kitsch cooking is that fun takes precedence over flavor. This means that a kitsch dish is always more enjoyable for your eyes than your tastebuds or, for that matter, your digestive tract. Kitsch cooking is not haute cuisine and it's not health food. Add to this the fact that Jews will always choose the processed form over the pure (hard to believe we were ever an agricultural people, but there it is) and you've got a recipe for bland, leaden cuisine. If you're a gourmand or a health nut, you're welcome to substitute fresh or higher-quality ingredients than we call for. But we frown on this for two reasons: 1) why put on airs?; and 2) any energy expended on procuring high-quality ingredients is energy you won't be directing toward sculpting the finished product into, say, an edible re-creation of Mount Sinai. Remember, you are what you eat. Would you rather be an unadorned portobello mushroom or a frilly piece of gefilte fish "Jewshi" (see page 45)? We thought so. *B'tayavon*.

the faith This book is not intended as a guide to Jewish practice or halachah (though it takes pains not to contradict it). It's just a guide to a more fun, stylish, Jewish life. We encourage you to improvise in ways that will better suit your spiritual and aesthetic expression. *L'Chaim*.

Starlet of David Sunglasses,
page 25

PART 1

EVERYDAY KITSCH

one snazzy jew

Unless you're Orthodox, living with your parents, or enrolled at Brandeis, it's easy to go day to day without affirming your Jewish identity. We miss the '70s, when everyone sported fist-sized Stars of David on nests of chest hair. Okay, we don't miss the chest hair. But we do encourage you to express your Jewishness on a daily basis in any way that suits you, and we're here to help. Your home and your clothes tell people who you are. These crafts tell people you're one snazzy Jew.

Give tzedakah hand-in-hand
with the one you love.

Neil Tzedakah Box

The *tzedakah* (charity) box, or *pushke,* is a staple of the Jewish home, though we suspect most of the change goes to parking meters. And while those turquoise Jewish National Fund tins have a certain nostalgia value, they're a little too ubiquitous for a do-it-yourself iconoclast like you. This tzedakah box might be more your speed. It honors Neil Sedaka, a Jewish mensch we would all do well to emulate. Just because we're kitschy doesn't mean we don't care. With such an inspirational box we think you'll find that breaking up (a dollar, that is) isn't hard to do.

YOU WILL NEED

Small box (A tin box with a slit in the top is ideal, but anything will do. We used an old Band-Aid tin.)

Acrylic craft paint and brush (optional)

A picture of Neil Sedaka

Good craft glue, such as Aleene's Tacky Glue

Rhinestones, beads, glitter, stickers, or whatever you want to decorate the box

א If your box is unsightly, you'll want to slap on a coat of acrylic craft paint before you start decorating. Allow to dry.

ב Glue your picture of Neil Sedaka to the box, then embellish to your heart's content.

ג Choose a charity for your tzedakah box proceeds. You may want to follow Mr. Sedaka's lead and contribute to Hadassah.

ד Every Erev Shabbat, Erev Yom Tov, and every time you do something really, really bad, empty your pocket change into the box.

The Miz-rock

A *mizrach* marks the eastern wall of your home. There's no law that says your mizrach can't be painted on black velvet. And there's certainly no law that says it can't be tacky. You could, for instance, paint a big-eyed Margaret Keane child in a yarmulke and tallis, praying in Jerusalem. Or perhaps you'd prefer a mizrach featuring fluffy kitties, gamboling in the Old City. Clowns, roses, Raggedy Ann dolls—paint whatever you like. But we do think a mizrach of dogs playing poker at the Western Wall is going too far. If you just can't bring yourself to paint something tasteless, you could paint something incredibly tasteful instead—say, a supermodel in a jewel-toned gown, with the Jerusalem sun setting behind her. Call it an Isaac Mizrach.

This mizrach features the King of all black velvet subjects: Elvis. Here we see him in the Holy Land, dressed to the nines in a stylish yarmulke and sporting kicky sidelocks. Though he wasn't Jewish, Elvis did play racquetball at the Memphis Jewish Community Center, so he is, in some sense, a member of the tribe. Viva!

YOU WILL NEED

16-by-24-inch piece of black velvet

Straight pins

Needle and thread or sewing machine

Piece of cardboard, 16 by 24 inches or bigger

Photo of Elvis

White chalk pencil (available at fabric stores)

Acrylic paints in various colors

Paintbrushes in various sizes

Fringe, ribbon, pom-pom trim, or whatever you want to decorate edges

א First you'll prepare your lovely velvet canvas. Turn edges of velvet ½ inch under all around and pin in place. Sew down with needle and thread or sewing machine. Once that's finished, pin velvet to cardboard to hold it in place while you paint.

ב Using your photo of Elvis as a reference, sketch out what you want to paint on the black velvet with white chalk pencil. It is difficult to get detail with the pencil on velvet, but do your best, and practice on velvet scraps if necessary.

ג Paint in your design. Painting on velvet is basically like painting on canvas, except that you can't wipe away your mistakes and it's a weird texture. Make sure you put the Hebrew word "mizrach" on there somewhere.

ד After the paint has dried, adorn your masterpiece with fringe, ribbon, pom-pom trim, or anything else that makes your Miz-rock rock harder.

Hang this snazzy number on the eastern wall of the rumpus room.

Celebrity Star of David Quilt

We've honored our favorite Jewish and gentile Davids with this fabulous quilted wall-hanging. If we'd had more room, we would have included nice Jewish boy David Lee Roth as well. You can include whatever Davids you like. David Bowie, David Schwimmer, David Copperfield, David Cassidy—knock yourself out.

This is a challenging project unless you're already a quilter. If you're not, see if you can get Mom to make it for you. Our mom made (and designed) this one for us. She reports that it was made all the more challenging by an iron that spit up on David Hasselhoff's face and ruined his picture, forcing her to start all over. Before you begin, you may want to make sure your iron doesn't have an aversion to Hasselhoff, too.

YOU WILL NEED

4 photos or digital photos of your favorite Davids, at least 8 x 8 inches

4 printer fabric sheets, inkjet transfer sheets, or color copier transfer sheets (available at fabric and craft stores)

½ yard white muslin (omit if using printer fabric sheets)

2½ yards of various accent fabrics

Sewing machine or needle and thread

1 roll quilt batting

1 yard backing fabric

א Transfer photos onto printer fabric sheets, or onto muslin using inkjet transfer sheets or color copier transfer sheets. Cut into hexagon shapes.

ב Cut twenty-four triangles out of accent fabric. Sew six triangles to each hexagon to form a Star of David. Cut the rest of the accent fabric and piece together quilt top as desired.

ג Cut a piece of batting the same size as your pieced quilt top. Cut the backing fabric to the same size. Mark center points of quilt top, batting, and backing. Line up the center points and pin all three pieces together. Baste. Quilt as desired or tie with embroidery thread.

ד Cut accent fabric into four strips for the border. Pin strips to raw edges of quilt and hand-sew in place.

Clockwise from top left: David Letterman, David Duchovny, Michelangelo's David (note the modest cover-up), and David Hasselhoff.

What's cuter than Ultra-Orthodox cats and dogs?

Merry Mezuzot

Mezuzot identify your home as Jewish. Shouldn't they identify your home as super-stylish, too? There aren't a lot of laws regarding the crafting of mezuzot. Nonetheless, campy irony feels out of place here. But cuteness and good cheer don't. These clay mezuzot will brighten your doorway as they remind you of your religious obligations. Now there's a mezuzah you'll want to kiss coming and going. For inexperienced potters and those of you who don't have a kiln in the basement, we provide the easy variation below.

YOU WILL NEED

8 ounces low-fire clay for each mezuzah

Fettling knife (a butter knife will also work)

Underglazes in a variety of colors

Paintbrushes in a variety of sizes

Cone 06 clear glaze

Klaf

א Wedge your clay and prepare a slab about 1 inch thick. Trace the shape of your mezuzah onto the clay and cut it out with your knife.

ב Turn your mezuzah over and hollow out the back to make room for the *klaf* (mezuzah scroll). Put a hole in the top and the bottom so you can hang it up.

ג After the clay has dried at least 24 hours, go Pop Art on your mezuzah and decorate it however you like. Just be sure to include the Hebrew letter *shin* on it somewhere.

ד Bisque fire to cone 04.

ה Apply a clear glaze and fire to cone 06. Once it's cool, insert the klaf and mount to your doorframe. Cute and kosher!

EASY VARIATION You can also make your mezuzah out of an oven-bake polymer clay like Fimo. You'll need about 2 ounces. Just shape it and bake as directed on package. Once it's cool, decorate it with acrylic craft paint. Let paint dry, then brush with a glossy clear acrylic sealer if you want a shiny finish.

Bragnets/Nagnets

Jewish homes have refrigerators for two reasons: 1) to keep the seltzer cold; and 2) to kvell over the kids' and grandkids' achievements. The refrigerator is like an ice-dispensing bulletin board, papered with report cards, blue ribbons, Nobel prizes, and whatever brings you *naches*. Now you can hold the awards up with magnets that will do the bragging for you and make your guests feel as inadequate as possible. What's the point of your kids achieving anything if you can't lord it over your friends?

If, however, you aren't expecting any guests, Bragnets become Nagnets. Velcro backing allows you to change the caption from "#1 Grandson" to "Would it kill you to phone your Zayde?" in seconds. The fridge is instantly transformed from a fountain of Fresca and praise to a cold museum of guilt and shame. The whole family will love the passive-aggressive fun!

YOU WILL NEED

Scissors or X-Acto knife

Craft foam in various colors

Good craft glue, such as Aleene's Tacky Glue

Lucite frame with magnetic backing (available at supermarkets, drugstores, and discount stores)

Adhesive-backed Velcro

Pen or printer

Piece of paper

Photo

א Using your scissors or an X-Acto knife, cut a frame out of craft foam. For a 3½-by-5-inch picture we cut a 5½-by-7-inch frame with a 3-by-4½-inch opening. Glue foam to Lucite frame and decorate with more foam if desired. Stick a small piece of Velcro where you want your caption to go.

ב Using a pen or printer, inscribe your caption on a piece of paper. Suggested captions for Bragnets: "My Son the Genius"; "My Daughter the Brain Surgeon"; "Nice Jewish Boy/Girl"; "#1 Balebusta"; or "That's Dr. Grandson to you." Suggested captions for Nagnets: "You never write, you never call"; "For this we pay $30,000 tuition?"; or "Nine months I carried you and this is how you act." Cut caption out and glue to a small piece of craft foam. Apply Velcro to back.

ג Slide photo into frame and stick on the refrigerator. If the photo's subject is in good graces, or if you're expecting company, stick on a flattering Bragnet caption. If the photo's subject is in the doghouse, give him or her a Nagnet caption. May s/he burn with shame every time s/he reaches for the orange juice.

Starlet of David Sunglasses

On our first trip to Florida, we were floored by the fashion. We'd been in high school plays. We lived next door to club kids. Still, in our entire lives, we'd never seen as many sequins as we saw on the bosoms of Bubbes at the early bird buffet.

These starlet-styled Star of David Sunglasses pay tribute to the Bubbes' fabulous fashion sense. They're super-stylish and they'll keep the Florida sun out of your eyes. If you want them extra-flashy, embellish with sequins and rhinestones. They'll look great with that sequined sweater you love so much. Who's behind those Foster Grants? One good-lookin' Jew.

YOU WILL NEED

Eyeglass repair kit (available at drugstores)

1 pair of cool shades

2 Star of David pendants (Available at bead stores. Look for good, heavy ones. You may want to steal them off a keychain, or make your own from polymer clay.)

Two 6-inch lengths of chain (Available at bead stores and hardware stores. Look for something lightweight with links about ⅛ to ¼ inch long.)

Needle-nose pliers

Using the miniature screwdriver in your eyeglass repair kit, remove the screws that hold the arms of your sunglasses to the frame so you are left with just the front of the sunglasses.

Attach the Star of David pendants to the lengths of chain using your needle-nose pliers.

Attach the chain and charms to the sunglass frames with the needle-nose pliers by attaching the first link of the chain to the eye where the arms used to screw in. Voila! The weight of the charms holds the sunglasses on, and you don't need to bother finding matching earrings. Shine on, you crazy diamond.

Patron Jew Votive Candles

Jews don't have saints—we have specialists. Instead of Lourdes, we have the Mayo Clinic. Instead of prophets, we have psychiatrists. We also have an endless supply of self-appointed martyrs, but that's another story.

For lost causes and cases despaired of, we turn to our chiropodists, our accountants, our internists. And who's to say they don't perform little miracles. The artful nose job, the larger-than-expected tax return, the speedily healed bunion—all these things are evidence of the divine in our daily lives. We honor our helpers and healers with these candles.

YOU WILL NEED

Strip of paper for label

Pen

Good craft glue, such as Aleene's Tacky Glue

Picture of your designated Jew

Tall votive candle in glass holder (available in most supermarkets)

Flat-back gems, beads, sequins, glitter, or whatever you want to decorate the candle

ℵ Choose an honorific title for your Patron Jew and inscribe it on a strip of paper to make a label: "Bernie, Patron Jew of Righteous Kvetching"; "Ira, Patron Jew of Angry Sciatic Nerves"; "Andrea, Patron Jew of Icy-Cold Tab."

ℶ Glue picture and label to candle.

ℷ Glue on flat-back gems, beads, sequins, glitter, or whatever you want. Allow glue to set.

ℸ Light candle whenever the intervention of your Patron Jew is desired.

The "Steppin' Out" Yarmulke

Our grandmother used to make yarmulkes from crushed yellow velvet and gold fringe for our father, a man so sartorially conservative he doesn't even own jeans. They looked more like lampshades than religious headgear, and they were fabulous. This sequined, betassled yarmulke is tribute to her designs. Great for nighttime services!

We encourage you to embellish yours in any way you see fit. The possibilities are endless. You could make it out of hair-like fun fur to cover a bald spot, or sew on synthetic sidelocks for an instant Ultra-Orthodox look. You could make one out of a picnic tablecloth and adorn it with plastic food and ants. Or you could make a black leather one and decorate it with studs. Put on your thinking cap and see what you come up with.

YOU WILL NEED

Yarmulke template (page 122)

Tracing paper

Scissors

¼ yard fancy fabric (We recommend anything crushed, flocked, or glittery. Upholstery is fine. Avoid knits—they are hard to sew, and, we think, just plain tacky.)

Straight pins

¼ yard lining fabric

Needle and thread

2 feet seam binding (optional)

2 feet fancy-shmancy trim

Sequins, rhinestones, tassels, embroidery thread, or whatever you want to decorate the yarmulke

א Copy template onto tracing paper and cut out. This will be your pattern.

ב Fold fancy fabric in half, then in half again, so you have a four-ply stack. Pin pattern to stack and cut out. You should end up with four separate pieces. Repeat with lining fabric.

ג Pin sides of two fancy fabric pieces together and sew, leaving a ¼-inch seam allowance. Repeat with other two fancy fabric pieces. At this point you should have two halves. Pin halves together and sew, leaving a ¼-inch seam allowance.

ד Repeat Step 3 with lining fabric.

ה Place lining inside yarmulke and pin in place with wrong-sides facing. If using seam binding, pin all around the bottom and sew together. Or, for a cleaner look, skip the seam biding and pin yarmulke and lining together with right-sides facing. Sew a seam all around, ¼ inch in, leaving the last inch open. Pull yarmulke right-side out through 1-inch opening. Topstitch, if desired. Then pin the fancy-shmancy trim around the bottom and sew down.

ו Now, decorate with your sequins, rhinestones, tassels, or embroidery. Don't let good taste hold you back. All those other poor suckers will be wearing drab black acetate, but you'll sparkle like a lampshade in a bordello.

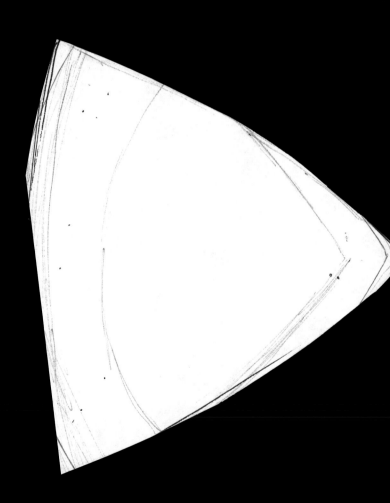

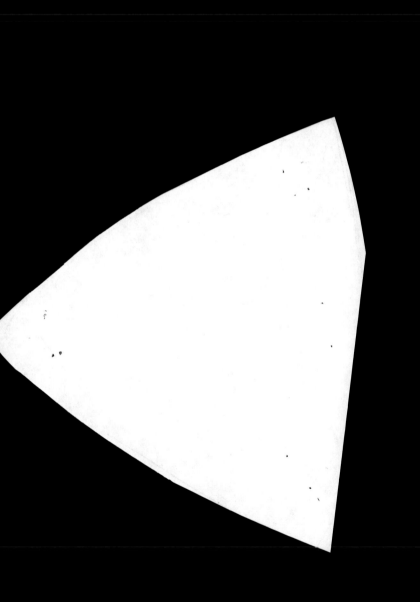

The Hippie Cowboy Yarmulke

The Funky Alien Yarmulke

The Puppet Yarmulke

The Carmen Miranda Yarmulke

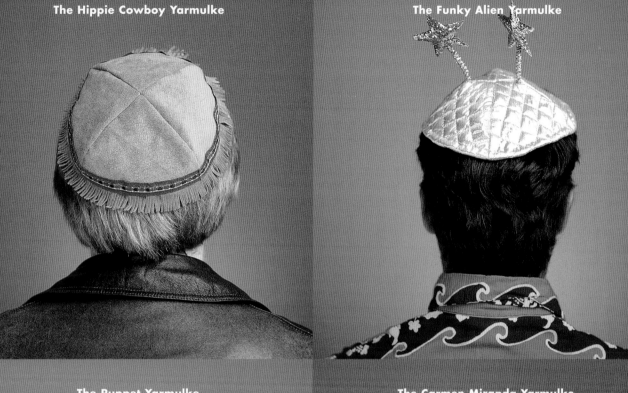

Pet Yarmulke

Your pets are Jewish, too. Our dog showed us he was Jewish shortly after we got him by vomiting pork. And our cat demonstrated his Jewishness by refusing to work on Shabbat.

Make your furry friends feel like part of the tribe with this tiny yarmulke. Pets love headgear! For the two seconds he allows it to stay on his head, it will be the funniest thing you've ever seen, worth all the time it took you to make it. Add an elastic chin strap to keep it on even the most active dogs and cats. This model is designed to perch in between his ears, but if you like, you could make it bigger and add ear-slits. And don't forget the alphabet beads—you know how pets like to have their names on everything.

YOU WILL NEED

Pet yarmulke template (page 122)

Tracing paper

Scissors

⅛ yard fabric (Anything will do, but try to pick something that will flatter your pet's coloring. Stay away from knits, which are tricky to sew.)

Straight pins

⅛ yard lining fabric

Needle and thread

1 foot seam binding (optional)

Alphabet beads (optional)

1 foot elastic (optional)

א Copy template onto tracing paper and cut out. This will be your pattern.

ב Fold yarmulke fabric in half, then in half again, so you have a four-ply stack. Pin pattern to stack and cut out. You should end up with four separate pieces. Repeat with lining fabric.

ג Pin sides of two yarmulke fabric pieces together and sew, leaving a ¼-inch seam allowance. Repeat with other two pieces of yarmulke fabric. At this point you should have two halves. Pin halves together and sew, leaving a ¼-inch seam allowance.

ד Repeat Step 3 with lining fabric.

ה Place lining inside yarmulke and pin in place with wrong-sides facing. If using seam binding, pin all around the bottom and sew together. Or, for a cleaner look, skip the seam biding and pin yarmulke and lining together with right-sides facing. Sew a seam all around, ¼ inch in, leaving the last inch open. Pull yarmulke right-side out through 1-inch opening. Top-stitch, if desired.

ו Sew on alphabet beads, if desired. Then, if you want a chin strap, measure your pet's chin from ear to ear. Cut a length of elastic one inch longer than this measurement and sew to each side of the yarmulke, leaving ½-inch allowance on each end. Pop the yarmulke on your pet's head. If he likes it, consider letting his sidelocks grow out.

**Remember to Bar Mitzvah
him when he's two.**

Ha'arnak sheli yafeh m'od!

Hebrew School Handbag

Hebrew school is the ten-year jail term all Jewish kids have to serve. Only our Catholic friends, who had to endure CCD, understood. It was fun for the first day, when we talked our teacher into teaching us Hebrew bathroom words, but after that we lost all interest. We still had to show up three afternoons a week. Oh, how the light blue Hebrew school *machberet* takes us back. It used to be the harbinger of boring afternoons imprisoned in a synagogue classroom. Now it's a darling accessory. *Ayzeh yofi!*

YOU WILL NEED

2 Hebrew lesson books

Clear contact paper

Hole punch

Thirty-six ½-inch black rubber grommets (available at hardware stores)

4 yards clear plastic tubing, ⅛ inch in diameter (available at hardware stores)

Super glue

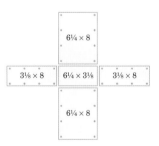

Remove the cover from one of the Hebrew lesson books and cut the front from the back, so you end up with two pieces, each 6¼ by 8 inches. Repeat with the second book, then cut the front in half to make two side panels, each 3⅛ by 8 inches. Use the remaining back cover to cut the piece for the bottom of the tote, 6¼ by 3⅛ inches.

Carefully lay these five pieces out on a sheet of contact paper, edges nearly touching, with the bottom piece in the middle as if you'd just cut open a paper bag (see diagram). Place another sheet of contact paper on top and smooth out to seal. Trim away excess contact paper, leaving a ¼-inch border.

Using your hole punch, make holes along the left and right edges of the front, the back, and the side panels, at 2½-inch intervals, so that there are four holes on each side of these four panels. Snap grommets into the holes you just made.

Cut sixteen 6-inch-long pieces of plastic tubing. Thread one of these pieces through the bottom holes of a side and front panel and tie in a knot. Snip away excess tubing. Continue with the rest of the pieces and the rest of the holes until the entire bag is sewn together.

Punch two more holes on both the front and back of the tote for the handle. Snap grommets in holes. Then make your handles by threading 2 feet of tubing through the holes you just made. Tie knots on the inside of the tote to secure handles. Dab a drop of super glue onto each of the knots for extra strength.

A belt like this is too good to waist. Thank you! I'll be here all week!

The Borscht Belt

For Jews, the Catskills were Camelot. Now that Jews spend their summers at spas and space camps, the closest we come to the Catskills is renting *Dirty Dancing*, aka The Best Movie of All Time. "Nobody puts Baby in a corner" remains our mantra to this day. Sigh.

The Catskills comedy circuit may be gone, but it lives on in this belt sure to inspire belly laughs. Brush up your cat skills and make one for yourself. Adorned with beads and miniature borscht vegetables, it's funny and fashionable. Great for beetniks.

YOU WILL NEED

Needle and thread

Scissors

2 feet of chain (Available at bead stores and hardware stores. Look for something lightweight and large, with links about 1-inch big.)

32 red seed beads

16 large red plastic beads

3 miniature ceramic, foam, or papier mâché beets (available at craft stores)

2 miniature ceramic, foam, or papier mâché carrots (available at craft stores)

4 miniature ceramic, foam, or papier mâché cabbages (available at craft stores)

Glue (optional)

7 Star of David pendants (available at bead stores)

Clasp

Cut a 12-inch length of thread. Loop thread through the second link of your chain. Bring both ends of the thread through the eye of the needle.

Thread on a seed bead, a large plastic bead, another seed bead, and a miniature vegetable. Knot off thread and pull loose end back through a bead to conceal. If you like, secure thread in place with a dab of glue.

Repeat beading on every other link, alternating miniature vegetables with Star of David pendants.

Attach clasp.

Don your belt and make lots of beet jokes ("I've got the beet!" "The beet goes on!" "Beet it!"). Can I get a rim shot?

Jewish American Princess Tiara

It's a stereotype. It's not pretty. But every once in a while, we all have our princess moments. In fact, we're sure that spending time with your relatives makes you feel like you were born into the Jewish Royal Family. You've got Sir Kvetchalot complaining about the hors d'oeuvres, the Contessa of Condescendia critiquing your hair, the Duke of Surl whining that he's schvitzing like a chazzer, while the Queen Mum herself insists, "Don't worry about me. I'll just freeze to death."

Let everyone know you need the royal treatment with some Hebrew headgear. As for the rest of them, let them eat sponge cake.

YOU WILL NEED

Plastic tiara

Princess decorations (We used little pink Princess phones, tiny Tab cans, Stars of David, and rhinestones. Search a cake decorating store or a craft store for supplies.)

Good craft glue, such as Aleene's Tacky Glue

א Glue your decorations to your tiara, and allow to set.

ב When glue is dry, don the tiara and command a loyal subject to bring you a spritzer.

Wear it proudly, Your Highness.

brunch party for the hard of herring

Next to monotheism, the greatest Jewish invention is brunch. Brunch is the most Jewish of meals. It is certainly our favorite. And frankly, it makes us proud to belong to a people whose inability to make it all the way to lunch led them to discover a new meal. But we have to ask: what's up with all the fish? Herring, whitefish, tuna, lox, gefilte . . . Good heavens. We're not Swedish. Do we really need that much fish before noon? We think not, and here's a fish-free brunch party menu to prove it.

MENU

One dozen assorted bagels
Rainbow of Shmears*
Gehakte Ayer*
Sliced tomatoes
Dill pickles
Brownies and cookies

Recipe follows

In traditional Judaism, a rainbow is considered a bad omen, but this one just portends good eatin'. (Rainbow of Shmears, page 40, and Gehakte Ayer, page 41.)

Rainbow of Shmears

Brighten your brunch with cream cheese spreads in a rainbow of flavors and colors. Also great for a Faygele Baygele Gay Pride Day Brunch. Make sweet or savory spreads or an assortment of both. If you're more interested in tints than tastes, skip the flavorings and simply color cream cheese with food coloring.

YOU WILL NEED

24 ounces cream cheese, softened

For red: 2 tablespoons strawberry jam or 2 tablespoons sundried tomatoes, finely chopped

For orange: 2 tablespoons marmalade or ½ teaspoon paprika

For yellow: 2 tablespoons lemon curd or 1 tablespoon Dijon mustard

For green: 2 tablespoons mint jelly or 1 tablespoon fresh green herbs, finely chopped, or ½ avocado, mashed

For blue: 2 tablespoons blueberry jam (Warning: this will be blue in name only. As we all know, blueberries actually tint things a purplish indigo. If you want true blue, reach for the food coloring.)

For purple: 2 tablespoons blackberry jam

א Separate cream cheese into six small bowls.

ב Stir respective flavorings into each bowl. If you want your shmear fine and fluffy, use a mixer or a hand blender. If you're making savory spreads, add salt to taste.

ג Arrange shmears in Roy G. Biv order and taste the rainbow.

SERVES 6

Gehakte Ayer

Gehakte Ayer sounds like you're clearing your throat, but it's actually a tasty egg pâté that can be sculpted into shapes. This morning you'll either sculpt it into a pot of gold (to be placed next to the Rainbow of Shmears) or the all-occasion favorite Star of David shape.

Gehakte Ayer was part of a roster of treats we often found in the graduate student lounge at Brandeis. The offerings consisted exclusively of mayonnaise-based salads that sat out all day. We liked to call it "the Salmonella Buffet." We hope your brunch is more appealing.

YOU WILL NEED

12 hard-boiled eggs, shelled

½ cup mayonnaise

2 tablespoons Dijon mustard

Dash Worcestershire sauce (optional)

Salt and pepper to taste

Combine all ingredients in a food processor and process until mixture is smooth and the consistency of pâté. Be careful not to overprocess—you'll end up with an unappetizing gluey liquid. If you don't have a food processor, a hand blender will also work.

To serve, you can sculpt the mixture into shapes, or serve in a great big mound.

SERVES 6

nosh party

It's been argued that Jews invented the appetizer. Jews are certainly its biggest fans, and we think it's high time we fete our favorite food. Plan a party around a pan-Asian pupu platter of tidbits adapted to Jewish tastes. If you also want to serve mainstream appetizer offerings like cheese and crackers and vegetables and dip, you can kitsch them up by arranging them in Star of David patterns and garnishing creatively. Try carving a radish into a dreidel shape or a carrot into a Torah pointer. Serve drinks that go well with salty snacks. Our favorite: The Jewish Princess (rum and Tab)—delish!

MENU

Vegetable Jew-Shoo*

Jewshi*

Jewmaki*

Cheese and cracker platter

Vegetable and dip platter

Recipe follows

Vegetable Jew-Shoo

The Jewish affinity for Chinese food is as deep as it is mysterious. Who knows why we love it so. Maybe it's because it's the only thing to eat on Christmas. Or maybe it's because Chinese restaurants indulge us by euphemistically listing pork as "meat" on the menu, allowing us to order it in blissful ignorance. As a grateful tribute, we've given our favorite Chinese dish an Ashkenazi makeover: it's been stripped of all spice and loaded down with fat. Mu shu meets matzo. Confucius say: *nu,* so eat some!

YOU WILL NEED

1 medium onion, finely chopped

5 tablespoons sesame oil

½ head small cabbage, finely shredded (or use a 12-ounce bag of shredded cabbage)

3 eggs, lightly beaten

Salt and pepper to taste

24 matzo crackers (or 2 matzos, broken into 24 squares)

In a large wok or skillet, sauté the onion in 2 tablespoons sesame oil over medium heat until translucent. Add cabbage and eggs and remaining 3 tablespoons sesame oil. Cook until cabbage is wilted and egg is cooked through. Season with salt and pepper.

Place a tablespoon of cabbage mixture on top of each matzo cracker and serve.

MAKES 24 PIECES

Serve with horseradish and
tell your friends it's Jewish wasabi.

Jewshi

We like sushi, but a people who fears contamination from all unpackaged foods is unlikely to eat raw fish. We've filled this sushi with gefilte fish instead. Why play food-poisoning roulette when you can have this sure bet?

YOU WILL NEED

2 cups sushi rice, rinsed until water runs clear (available at most supermarkets and at Asian markets)

2 cups water

3½ tablespoons rice vinegar

1 tablespoon sugar

1 teaspoon salt (optional)

4 sheets nori seaweed (available in the international aisle of most supermarkets and at Asian markets)

28-ounce jar gefilte fish, cut in ¼-by-¼-by-3-inch strips

4-ounce jar horseradish

א In a medium saucepan, combine rice and water over medium heat. Cover and bring to a boil. Reduce heat and cook until rice is tender and water is absorbed, about 15 to 20 minutes. Remove from heat and let rice stand, covered, for 10 minutes.

ב Combine vinegar, sugar, and salt, if desired, in a small bowl and stir until sugar is dissolved (microwaving the mixture for 30 seconds or so will help).

ג Transfer rice to a large bowl and stir in vinegar mixture.

ד Now, you'll start assembling the sushi. A bamboo sushi mat (available at Asian markets and kitchen stores) will make the job easier, but you can manage without one. Lay a sheet of plastic wrap or wax paper on your sushi mat, if you're using one. Place a sheet of seaweed on top. Spread a layer of rice on seaweed, about ¼ inch thick. Lay a strip of gefilte fish down the right side.

ה Carefully roll up the sheet from right to left. Press ends together. Remove bamboo mat and plastic wrap or wax paper. Cut roll into 1-inch-thick slices. Repeat until all ingredients are used up.

ו Serve with dollops of horseradish.

MAKES ABOUT 32 PIECES

Jewmaki

Rumaki makes us think of Lily Pulitzer shifts, highballs on the lanai, and treyf so good it's worth sinning for. Here is our kosher version of the '60s favorite canapé. We've replaced the traditional bacon and chicken liver with the kosher standbys lox and cream cheese. But if you're a purist, you could use soy bacon and the Mock Chopped Liver (see page 60) instead.

YOU WILL NEED

4 ounces cream cheese, softened

1 tablespoon soy sauce

24 water chestnuts (the culinarily adventurous, dentally timid, or gastrointestinally challenged can substitute 24 pitted prunes for an altogether different taste sensation)

6 ounces lox, cut into ½-by-4-inch strips

24 cocktail toothpicks

א In a small bowl, combine cream cheese and soy sauce. Mix well.

ב Top each water chestnut with ½ teaspoon cream cheese mixture (if you're using prunes instead, slit prunes and stuff cream cheese inside).

ג Wrap each water chestnut in a strip of lox and secure with a cocktail toothpick.

MAKES 24 PIECES

These little tidbits got us feeling so festive we were inspired to adorn them with Hanukkah flags, but you could try paper umbrellas or frilly picks for the off-season.

Can Can Candlesticks,
page 50

PART 2

SHABBAT

accessorize, accessorize, accessorize

Shabbat is the best day of the week because it has the most accessories. Kiddush cups, candlesticks, spice boxes—it's got it all. If Shabbat were a person she'd be the most popular girl in school.

We love Shabbat because it provides an occasion for a big festive dinner party every week. To keep things fun and fresh, we like themes. Some of our favorites: Friday Night Fever Disco Dinner, Black Sabbath Heavy Metal Meal, Hippie Dippie Shabbat (featuring *The Moosewood Cookbook*'s "Soy Gevalt"), Siouxie Sabbath Goth Get-Together, Cowboy Shabbat on the Range, Shabbat with the Stars (featuring recipes from our '70s *Celebrity Kosher Cookbook*), or Southern Belle Shabbat (featuring recipes from *Mazel Tov, Y'all*). We've been toying with the idea of a Hobbit Shabbat, but we don't look good in burlap and we don't fancy toadstools much. We're sure you'll come up with some fabulous ideas of your own. Here are some to get you started.

Can Can Candlesticks

Only in a Jewish home will you find fine china and Coke cans on the same table. Maybe it's because we can't drink milk with our meat meals. Maybe it's because we share a terrible sweet tooth. Or maybe it's because nothing washes a pastrami sandwich down like a Dr. Brown's. Whatever the reason, our affection for soda pop is longstanding and sure. Our mother tells us that when she was in college, all the sorority girls clamored for invitations to the Jewish fraternity for dinner—it was the only house that served soda instead of milk. We honor this affinity with these Can Can Candlesticks. Close observers will see we've incorporated two kinds of cans you'll never find in a Jewish home: 1) non-diet soda; and 2) beer. Beer-can crafts were an extravaganza of kitsch in the '60s and '70s. It was an extravaganza that Jews didn't join in much. We're just not big beer drinkers. But now that we have our own kitschy beer (He'Brew, the Chosen Beer), we figure it's okay to put beer cans into our crafts. We've used Budweiser cans because they're a kitsch classic, and because He'Brew only comes in bottles. But you can use any can you like. Löwenbräu seems appropriate, since Shabbat Is Kind of Special. As for sodas, Tab, Fresca, or any soda can will work as well. We also recommend Coca-Cola, since Shabbat Is the Pause that Refreshes.

א If you want to paint the two cans that will serve as your sconces, do it now. You may want to sand the cans a bit first. Paint cans with acrylic craft paint and a foam brush. Allow to dry.

ב Put on your work gloves and your protective eyewear. Using the can opener, remove the tops of all six of the cans. If the tops of the cans curve in, use tin snips or scissors to cut the curved ½ inch or so off.

ג Cut out a 3½-by-3½-inch panel from the front of the two cans that will serve as your sconces. Scallop bottom edge if desired. Then cut graduated fringes ⅛ inch thick and 2 inches long all the way around the rest of these two cans. Using your needle-nose pliers, curl each fringe. Then, if you like, you can decorate with flat-back rhinestones and glue.

YOU WILL NEED

6 empty aluminum cans, clean and dry

Sand paper (optional)

Acrylic craft paint (optional)

Foam brush (optional)

Work gloves

Protective eyewear

Can opener

Tin snips or good strong scissors

Needle-nose pliers

Flat-back rhinestones (optional)

Good nonflammable craft glue, such as Aleene's Tacky Glue

Plain store-bought candleholders

Electrical tape (optional)

Using the can opener, remove the bottoms of the remaining four cans. Cut down the side with scissors and flatten cans out. From the flattened cans, cut two panels that are just a little shorter than your store-bought candlesticks and 4½ inches wide. Then cut four Stars of David, 3 inches across, from flattened cans. In the center of each star, cut a circle with a ⅞-inch diameter.

Put store-bought candleholders through these circles so the Stars of David frame the cup and the base of each candleholder (you may need to disassemble the candleholder to do this). Then wrap the panels you just cut around candleholders and glue in place with good, nonflammable craft glue. Or, if glue won't do the trick, secure panels with some artfully concealed electrical tape.

Place your newly decorated store-bought candlesticks inside the fringed cans.

Pop open a cold one and admire your work.

The Rose Kiddush Cup

We hold the kiddush cup with five fingers reaching upward to recall a rose, which symbolizes the people of Israel, our longing for heaven, and perfection. Why not drive the point home by making a rose-shaped kiddush cup? And why not run the point into the ground by decorating your kiddush cup with the ultimate rose, Miss Bette Midler? Divine.

YOU WILL NEED

2 pounds low-fire clay

Fettling knife (a butter knife will also work)

Underglazes in a variety of colors

Paintbrushes in a variety of sizes

Photo of Bette Midler

Cone 06 clear glaze

א Wedge your clay and pinch out a cup about 4 inches tall, using the knife as necessary. Form 5 rose petals out of clay and attach them around the cup to form a rose shape.

ב Roll out a coil of clay about ¾ inch thick and attach to bottom of cup. Make a base for the chalice and attach to the bottom of the coil.

ג After the clay has dried, paint Bette's likeness on your kiddush cup with the underglazes, using her photo as a reference. We think she looks good smack dab in the middle of the cup.

ד Bisque fire to cone 04.

ה Apply a clear glaze and fire to cone 06. *L'Chaim!*

EASY VARIATION You could also make your kiddush cup from an oven-bake polymer clay. Follow steps 1 and 2, using polymer clay instead of low-fire clay (you'll need about a pound). Bake according to package directions. When the cup is cool, decorate with acrylic craft paint. Let the paint dry, then brush with a glossy clear acrylic sealer if you want a shiny finish. *Make sure* your clay, your paint, and your sealer are all approved for contact with food (Fimo and Sculpey are not). If they don't say they're food-safe on the label, they probably aren't. If you can't find food-safe products, just use your cup for decorative purposes.

Hollywood Challah Cover

One of our favorite things about Judaism is that it takes the feelings of inanimate objects into account. We light Hanukkah candles from left to right so that each one gets a chance to be first. We kiss prayerbooks when we drop them. And we cover the challah so it won't feel ashamed when we bless the wine. Here's a cover that will make any challah feel like a movie star. It's made from panty hose, which seems fitting, since challah goes straight to your thighs. We made ours out of frumpy support hose. But if you're feeling saucy, feel free to make yours out of fishnets.

YOU WILL NEED

Four 12-inch lengths of support hose (the heavier, the better—choose a *denier* your grand-mother would wear)

Polyfill stuffing

Needle and thread

Black seed beads

13-by-13-inch square of black velvet

Straight pins

4 feet gold pom-pom trim

Beads, rhinestones, or whatever you'd like to decorate the cover (optional)

א First you'll make your support-hose challah. Knot ends of four lengths of support hose together. Stuff each length with polyfill until puffy. Braid stuffed support hose and knot other ends together. Sew black seed beads on top.

ב Next, you'll prepare the cover itself. Take your velvet square and turn ½ inch under all around, to make a 12-by-12-inch finished square. Pin gold pom-pom trim in place along the edges. Sew down all around.

ג Center support-hose challah on velvet square and sew in place, concealing hosiery ends under challah. If you like, you can decorate further with beads and rhinestones.

We usually serve two challot on Shabbat.
Here we just used one, because we wanted a sleek look.

Shabbos Queen Challah Hairdo Plate

It's traditional to braid challah. We say, why stop there? Bake your challah in the shape of a chignon, a bouffant, a beehive (especially nice to serve with honey on Rosh Hashanah), a French twist, a *That Girl* flip, or (kosher) pigtails. Serve on our special plate, adorned with a portrait of the traditional Shabbos Queen. Change her hairdo every week!

YOU WILL NEED

4 pounds low-fire clay

Fettling knife (a butter knife will also work)

Underglazes in a variety of colors

Paintbrushes in a variety of sizes

Cone 06 clear glaze

נ Wedge your clay and prepare a ¾-inch-thick slab, using the knife as necessary.

ב Cut your slab into an 18-by-9-inch rectangle and curl the edges up to form a lip. If you want a 3-D Shabbos Queen, sculpt a three-dimensional head (about one inch thick) and attach to the center of the plate. This way, the ceramic head and the challah hairdo will be on equal planes. If you're happy with 2-D, just stick with a plain plate for now. Allow plate to dry.

ג Using your underglazes, paint a dashing lady with fantastic hair to serve as inspiration for the challah hairdos.

ד Bisque fire to cone 04.

ה Apply a clear glaze and fire to cone 06.

EASY VARIATION If you don't happen to have a kiln in your basement (and if you're Jewish, you probably don't), this is a great project to do at a paint-your-own pottery joint. You could also just paint a store-bought platter at home, but if you do, *make sure* your paint is approved for contact with food. If it doesn't say it's food-safe on the label, it probably isn't. If you can't find food-safe products, just use your platter for decorative purposes.

Spice Girls Spice Box

We mark the end of Shabbat with the havdalah ceremony. "Havdalah" means separation, and with their breakups and divorces, we figure the Spice Girls know a few things about that. At havdalah we say goodbye to Shabbat with *besamim,* sweet spices that remind us of the sweetness of Shabbat. Here's a besamim box with Girl Power.

YOU WILL NEED

Small box

Pictures of the Spice Girls (with or without Ginger)

Good craft glue, such as Aleene's Tacky Glue

Rhinestones, sequins, glitter, stickers, or whatever you want to decorate the box

Cinnamon sticks, cloves, whole nutmeg, or whatever you want to smell

א This is a one-note project: just glue some Spice Girls pictures to your box, then decorate with rhinestones, sequins, glitter, and stickers as you see fit.

ב Fill box with spices to sniff during havdalah. *Zig ah zig ahhhhh.*

Sing "Eliahu Ha Navi"
to the tune of "Wannabe!"

shabbette! a dinner tribute to bette midler

If you're asking, "why Bette Midler?" then you haven't been paying attention. The Divine Miss M embodies Judaikitsch at its perfect pinnacle. Below are recipes from Shabbette!, the extravaganza we planned to unveil our Rose Kiddush Cup (see page 52). Between courses we suggest you act out scenes from her movies. You may also want to give a drosh on your favorite Midler monologue. Afterward, sing Birkat Hamazon to the tune of "You Gotta Have Friends" or "Wind Beneath My Wings." We only hope she knows that she's our hero.

MENU

Boogie Woogie Kugel*

Mock Chopped Liver*

Challah

Baked Chicken (make Baked Tempeh for vegetarians)

Green Salad

Berry Manilow*

*Recipe follows

Boogie Woogie Kugel

Kugel is the most traditional of Jewish foods. Homey and satisfying, it transforms humble everyday ingredients into a creation special enough for Shabbat. We think this version is extra-special. It's a casserole tribute to Miss Midler's underrated film, *For the Boys.* Like Miss Midler, it's a little spicy.

YOU WILL NEED

6 large potatoes, peeled and grated

1 onion, grated

3 eggs, lightly beaten

⅓ cup oil

2 tablespoons matzo meal

2 tablespoons cream-style horseradish

Salt and pepper to taste

Preheat oven to 400°F and liberally grease a casserole dish or a 9-by-9-inch baking dish.

In a large bowl, combine potatoes, onion, and eggs. Mix well, then add oil, matzo meal, horseradish, salt, and pepper.

Pour mixture into casserole dish or Pyrex pan. Bake for an hour and fifteen minutes or until golden brown.

SERVES 6

Mock Chopped Liver

It's traditional to serve chopped liver on Shabbat. But we have our own tradition, which is to never, ever eat liver. We prefer this delicious spread made from lentils, walnuts, and onion. The best part: it can be sculpted into shapes.

YOU WILL NEED

3 cups water

2 cubes of mock chicken or
   vegetable bouillon

1 cup lentils

1 onion, chopped

2 tablespoons oil or margarine

2 cups walnuts, chopped

4 eggs, hard-boiled

Salt and pepper to taste

Matzo shards or crackers

א In a saucepan, bring water to a boil. Add bouillon and lentils. Cover and cook 30 minutes or until tender, adding more water if necessary. Strain.

ב While the lentils cook, combine onion and oil or margarine in a skillet and sauté over medium heat until onion is translucent.

ג In a food processor, combine lentils, onion, walnuts, and hard-boiled eggs. Process until smooth. If you don't have a food processor, a hand blender will also work. Season with salt and pepper. Chill.

ד Sculpt or serve in a great big mound. Garnish with matzo shards or crackers.

SERVES 6 BIG FRESSERS

Some say love, it is a flower.
I say love, it is a chopped liver sculpture.

Berry Manilow

Traditionally known as kissel, we've renamed this delicious Russian raspberry pudding after Miss Midler's former accompanist, because, like Barry Manilow, it's sweet and smooth. Our grandmother always made it for special occasions. It was so good that even when we were beached on the rug next to the dinner table with our waistbands unbuttoned, we'd still manage to rally and put away a couple helpings. It's Jewish Jell-O and we think you'll agree, there's always room for kissel.

YOU WILL NEED

Four 12-ounce packages of frozen raspberries

1⅓ cup water

1 cup superfine sugar

¼ cup cornstarch dissolved in 6 tablespoons water

¾ cup light cream, crème fraîche, or whipped cream (for fleishig meals, use a pareve nondairy substitute)

א In a large pot, combine raspberries and water over medium heat. Bring to a boil, then reduce heat. Simmer until berries are soft.

ב Pass berries through a sieve to remove seeds. Or, if you want texture, just leave them as is. Add sugar.

ג Return the mixture to the stove over a medium flame. Add cornstarch solution. Bring to a boil.

ד Cover mixture and allow to cool to room temperature. Transfer to refrigerator. Serve cold with a drizzle of light cream, crème fraîche, whipped cream, or your nondairy substitute.

SERVES 6

As served at the
Copacabana.

We found this piñata in a rural supermarket's Cinco de Mayo display. Note the upside-down and backwards Hebrew letters—the perfect centerpiece for our Rosh Mexicana dinner.

ROSH HAShANAH

i'm too sexy for my shul

Rosh Hashanah is the only time most Jews go to synagogue, and we dress as though it were the Oscars. Thus, it's become known as the fashion show of the Jewish calendar. It's that and so much more. It's the time of year we try to be our best in every way and that means sending the best greetings (L'Shana Tova Clip Art Cards, see page 67), crafting the best tchotchkes (Jewish Time Zones Clock, see page 69), and throwing the best get-togethers.

Rosh Hashanah is highly holy, of course, but it's not somber. It's the occasion for our biggest annual dinner party. One year it was Rosh Italiana, and we ate Rosh Lasagne. Another year, it was Rosh HaShania, a country-western tribute to Shania Twain. Most recently it was Russia Shanah, a vodka and zakuskie buffet. But our favorite was Rosh Mexicana, a South-of-the-Border fiesta. We served Kosher Cowgirl Casserole (see page 70), Tamaligi (see page 71), and Hava Tequila Pie (see page 72). We partied like it was 5761.

**It must be a mitzvah
to look this good.**

**Sometimes it's fun
to be Jewish.**

**Sometimes,
not so much.**

**Mom lied.
It doesn't say anything about
Corvettes being forbidden in here.**

Swing, brother!

L'Shana Tova Clip Art Cards

Now you don't need artistic skills to create your own cards—you just need a smart-aleck attitude and a book of clip art. Write your own snarky captions for prefab illustrations to create one-of-a-kind greetings. Remember, nothing says "Happy New Year" like sarcasm!

These directions will produce ten cards. If you have more than ten friends you will need more supplies. Be sure to send cards to your shut-in relatives and the needy friends you sometimes avoid. You want to rack up all the mitzvot you can before Yom Kippur. May you be signed, sealed, and delivered into the Book of Life.

YOU WILL NEED

Book of Jewish clip art (available at craft stores)

Scissors

11 pieces of 6-by-9-inch stationery

Glue stick

Pen or printer and paper scraps

10 envelopes

ℵ Leaf through your book of clip art and choose your favorite subject: Bar Mitzvah boy, apple and honey platter, shofar-tooting rabbi, or whatever you like. Cut the picture out or, if you want to keep your book intact, make a photocopy to cut up instead.

ℶ Fold a piece of stationery in half and glue your clip art cutout to the front. Then write or print a caption on a scrap of paper to glue underneath. Go for smirky commentary or corny greetings: "You're the apple of my eye, honey!"; "We're blowing a blast of L'Shana Tova greetings your way!"; etc.

ℷ Photocopy your creation onto 10 sheets of stationery. Fold sheets in half to make cards.

ℸ Write a nice message inside, then pop cards in envelopes and send them off to the whole mishpocheh.

Go to sleep already.

The hours you keep, it's a shande.

You with the sleeping in.

I told you so. I'll get the bicarbonate.

You're wearing that?

You eat that now, you'll have heartburn all night.

How about a nice piece of fruit?

Are you trying to give me a heart attack?

Don't eat now, you'll spoil your dinner.

I'll be up all night worrying about you.

We can still make the Early Bird Special.

You're going out? On a weeknight?

Tick. Tock. You're one minute closer to death.

Jewish Time Zones Clock

The High Holidays return us to sacred time. Why not make a clock that will remind you of Jewish time all year long?

Jewish time has many different zones. The first is S.J.T. (Standard Jewish Time). This is the same as Standard Italian Time, Standard Irish Time, Standard Latin Time, etc. All ethnic groups think they run later than everyone else, and Jews are no exception. The S.J.T. clock reads "5 minutes late, 10 minutes late, 15 minutes late," and so on. Then there's A.J.T. (Approximate Jewish Time), the time zone all fathers operate in, especially on road trips. The A.J.T. hours are as follows: "One-ish. Two-ish. Three-ish. You want exact time, you call NASA. What are you bugging me for?" But the Greenwich mean of Jewish time is J.M.T., or Jewish Mother Time. Instead of seconds, minutes, and hours, J.M.T. divides the day into anxieties, worries, and dire warnings, all ticking toward an impending doom. We've made our J.M.T. clock with an extra-loud motor, so not a second goes by without us contemplating our mortality. It seems especially appropriate this time of year.

YOU WILL NEED

10-inch plastic wall clock (Nothing fancy. The best kind can be bought for a few shekels at a drugstore like Walgreens.)

Butter knife

Stiff paper

Pencil

Scissors and/or X-Acto knife

Pen or printer

Glue stick (optional)

Stickers (optional)

א Carefully remove the clear plastic cover of the clock. If it doesn't pop out easily, you should be able to jimmy it off by wedging a butter knife between the cover and the rim of the clock. It's easy to crack both the cover and the rim, so don't force it. Set cover aside. Gently remove the clock hands and paper clock-face and set aside.

ב Trace around the paper clock-face you just removed onto stiff paper. Cut circle out. Using the paper clock-face as a guide, lightly mark the placement of the numbers onto the stiff-paper circle. Mark the center on the stiff-paper circle and cut out a small hole to fit around the clock pin. An X-Acto makes this easier.

ג Inscribe your paper circle with the hours in S.J.T., A.J.T., or J.M.T. as pictured. Write directly on the circle or glue print-outs on with glue stick. If you like, decorate with some stickers.

ד Install stiff-paper circle into the clock base, making sure 12 o'clock is at the top. Replace clock hands and plastic cover.

Kosher Cowgirl Casserole

Who says Hebrew and habaneros don't mix? Part enchilada and part Latin lasagne, this dish is Tex-Mex without the treyf. Olé!

YOU WILL NEED

12 corn tortillas, torn into
  2-by-2-inch pieces

15-ounce can black beans,
  strained

15-ounce can corn, strained

19-ounce can enchilada sauce

2 cups Monterey Jack cheese,
  grated

3 to 4 tomatoes, chopped

3 to 4 green onions, chopped

1 cup sour cream

6-ounce can black olives, strained
  and sliced

א Preheat oven to 350°F. Grease a 9-by-13-inch baking dish.

ב Line bottom of pan with half the tortilla pieces. Top with half the beans, half the corn, half the sauce, half the cheese, half the tomatoes, and half the green onions. Next, layer on the rest of the tortilla pieces. Top with the rest of the beans, corn, sauce, cheese, tomatoes, and green onions. Cover with foil.

ג Bake for 30 minutes. Remove foil and bake 15 more minutes, or until cheese starts to brown.

ד Serve hot from the chuckwagon with dollops of sour cream and a sprinkling of sliced olives.

SERVES 8

Tamaligi

Mamaligi is Jewish cornmeal porridge. When mamaligi meets sweet corn tamale fixin's, the result is Hebrew hot stuff.

This is one of our favorite side dishes. It is very, very rich, and very, very sweet. It's the closest we've come to getting frosting classified as a side dish. ¡Qué rico!

YOU WILL NEED

4 cups water

2 cups masa harina flour (Check the international aisle at the supermarket. If there's none to be had, you can substitute cornmeal.)

1 cup sugar

1 teaspoon salt

1 cup margarine

2 cups corn, canned, frozen, or fresh

¾ teaspoon baking powder

א Preheat oven to 275°F. Grease a 9-by-13-inch baking dish.

ב In a large saucepan, bring water to a boil. Add masa flour, sugar, salt, and margarine and cook until mixture thickens and pulls away from the sides of the pan (about 10 minutes). Remove from heat and stir in corn and baking powder.

ג Transfer mixture to baking dish. Bake for 45 minutes. Serve hot.

SERVES 8

Hava Tequila Pie

It's a salty snack, a dessert, and a drink in one. It's a margarita you can eat with a fork. It's Hava Tequila Pie and it's so delicious, you'll hava two slices.

Our mother used to serve a nonalcoholic variation of this recipe that, to her great annoyance, we referred to as "White Trash Pie." But we think even Mom will agree that the addition of tequila classes it up ever so much.

YOU WILL NEED

1½ cups pretzels, finely crushed

⅔ cup butter or margarine, melted

¼ cup sugar

4 cups vanilla ice cream, softened

½ cup frozen limeade concentrate, thawed

¼ cup tequila

2 tablespoons triple sec

In a medium bowl, combine pretzels, butter or margarine, and sugar. Press mixture into a 9-inch pie plate to form a crust.

In a large bowl, stir together ice cream, limeade, tequila, and triple sec. Pour into pie crust. Freeze 4 hours or until firm.

SERVES 8

That's not a pig in the background—it's a pink cow.

It's the Malibu Dream Sukkah!
(Dolls sold separately.)

SUKKOT high camp

Sukkot is the holiday a child would imagine. You get to spend the whole week camping out in a fort! And you are literally commanded to be happy!

Nothing makes us happier than a theme party. Sukkot really lends itself to a Gilligan's Island/Tiki motif. Make a Hawaiian hut–styled sukkah from rush mats, palm fronds, and Polynesian decorations. Craft a miniature Tabletop South Sea Sukkah (see page 76) for a centerpiece. Then invite the whole tribe over for a Sukkot Luau. Serve Poi Vey Pineapple Mold (see page 79), Tropical Tsimmes (see page 77), Castaway Carrot Candy (see page 80), and fancy umbrella drinks. Call it the Bali Hai Holidays.

Your party will be super-fun or sadly misguided, depending on how late Sukkot falls and where you live. It can be hard to feel tropical about a late-October Sukkot in Buffalo. But that's part of the fun, so buck up and enjoy. You're sure to walk away with some great tales, or, if you're really lucky, a nice tan.

Tabletop South Sea Sukkah

In the 1940s, a rabbi started a movement to get apartment-dwelling Jews to build minia-ture tabletop sukkahs. It didn't really catch on. It seems Jews would rather reserve pre-cious table space for things you can actually eat. But we love the idea. It's a centerpiece *and* a dollhouse. We went with a South Sea theme to suit our Sukkot Luau, but you may decorate your tabletop sukkah in any way you see fit. Be sure to put some action figures inside to play with when things get dull. You can have them act out Biblical stories or great moments in your own family's history, like "The Time Irving Ruined Our Trip to Hawaii" or "How Stephanie's Tantrum Almost Caused a Car Accident." Good times.

YOU WILL NEED

Cardboard

Scissors

Packing tape

Hot glue gun or good craft glue, such as Aleene's Tacky Glue

½ yard fabric or pretty paper

3 sushi mats

Astroturf

Palm leaves (real or artificial)

Decorations (furniture, tiny fruits and flowers, or whatever you like)

Action figures (optional)

א Cut cardboard into three pieces, each the same size as a sushi mat. Tape the pieces together to make a jointed frame. Using a hot glue gun or good craft glue, glue fabric or paper to one side, and the sushi mats to the other.

ב Lay down a carpet of Astroturf.

ג Make a roof by balancing palm leaves on the top. Decorate sukkah how-ever you like. Place action figures inside, if desired, and let the festivities begin.

Tropical Tsimmes

Of all the traditional Jewish dishes, tsimmes is our favorite. There are two reasons: 1) sugar; and 2) fat. Rich and satisfying, it's usually made with brisket, but we prefer a version that's more sweet than savory. Here's our recipe for a traditional treat with a tropical twist. Because we don't actually live in a tropical climate, and hence are spared the tyranny of bikinis, this recipe contains what is admittedly a shocking amount of sugar and margarine. You can cut down on either or both, if you like, substituting a splash of orange juice. But we don't recommend it. You're looking too thin as it is.

YOU WILL NEED

4 large sweet potatoes, baked, peeled, and chunked

½ cup dates, coarsely chopped

½ cup prunes, coarsely chopped

½ cup dried apricots, coarsely chopped

1 cup pineapple chunks

⅓ cup flaked sweetened coconut

2 carrots, peeled, sliced, and boiled (Optional. Tradition demands carrots, but our palates demand leaving them out. You may add them if you like.)

Splash of orange juice (optional)

½ cup margarine, cubed

1 cup brown sugar

Preheat oven to 300°F. Grease a casserole dish or 9-by-13-inch Pyrex baking dish.

In a large bowl, combine sweet potatoes, dates, prunes, apricots, pineapple, coconut, and carrots and orange juice, if using. Mix well.

Transfer mixture to casserole dish or Pyrex pan. Top with margarine and brown sugar.

Bake for 30 minutes.

SERVES 8

Looks like a pineapple—
tastes like a liver!

Poi Vey Pineapple Mold

Doesn't everything taste better when it's shaped like a pineapple? Okay, no. But it doesn't taste worse. This mock chopped liver makes a pareve pineapple, but if you're having a milchig meal, you can mold your pineapple out of cheese dip instead. Whichever you use, tell your friends it's a secret island substance called "poi vey."

YOU WILL NEED

2 batches mock chopped liver (page 60)

Butter knife

1 jar green olives, sliced (optional)

Leafy top of a pineapple

א Dump the chopped liver on your serving platter and sculpt into the shape of a pineapple.

ב With a butter knife, score a diamond pattern into the liver. If you like, you can place an olive slice in the center of each diamond.

ג Crown your mold with the leafy top of a pineapple and refrigerate until you're ready to serve.

SERVES 8 TO 12

Castaway Carrot Candy

We've noticed that the more kosher the dinner, the sweeter the vegetable side dish. Peas, corn, cabbage, beets, beans, and even Brussels sprouts are served sugared and honeyed. But nothing gets the sweet treatment like carrots. It's the peculiar provenance of Jewish cooking to regard carrots as a dessert. Carrot pudding, carrot cake, and worst of all, carrot candy—known as ingberlach—are all traditional Jewish dishes. It's especially traditional to make them this time of year. The recipe below is basically carrot fudge and should only be served to children and adults of whom you're not very fond. It doesn't have any leaven in it, so you can punish bad castaways during Passover, too.

YOU WILL NEED

2 pounds carrots, peeled and chopped

3¾ cups sugar, plus more for sprinkling

1½ teaspoons ground ginger

¾ teaspoon cinnamon

¼ cup lemon juice

¼ cup orange juice

¾ cup blanched almonds, finely chopped or ground (optional)

א In a large saucepan, boil carrots until tender. Drain. Return carrots to saucepan and mash.

ב Add 3¾ cups sugar, ginger, cinnamon, lemon juice, orange juice, and almonds, if using, to carrots. Cook over low heat 10 to 20 minutes, or until thick, stirring occasionally.

ג Dust a cutting board with sugar. Pour carrot mixture over it. Sprinkle top of mixture with more sugar. Allow to harden a bit, then cut or mold into shapes. Top each terrifying morsel with a paper parasol.

MAKES 24 CANDIES

Think of it as an immunity challenge.

We say, "Take a load off" with
our festive couch menorah (page 85).

HANUKKAH

PART 5

burn, baby, burn

Hanukkah starts off fun, but burns out fast. It can be hard to sustain the excitement for eight days, especially when the presents get lamer each night. Our non-Jewish friends, who were always so jealous that we got presents for eight whole days, never saw our scowling faces as we opened our booty of travel-size shampoo bottles, ballpoint pens, and keychains on the eighth evening. We are convinced that all eighth-night gifts come from the junk drawer.

To make the fun last for eight miraculous nights, you'll need to throw a really spectacular shindig. We suggest a Viva Las Vegas party. After all, it's the Festival of Lights, celebrated with fried food and gambling, and the presents are a total crapshoot. How Vegas can you get? Serve glitzy buffet fare like Latke Gravlax (see page 89) and Las Veggies Menorah Salad (see page 90). Don your Hanukkah Headband (see page 88), blaze up the Mah-Jongg Menorah (see page 87), and say oy to the world. Swing, baby!

If only we all had nine mouths each—
imagine how many latkes you could eat.

Make-Your-Own Menorah

It's easy to make your own menorah in any shape you like. We made menorot that reflect our favorite hobbies: lounging on the couch and cramming things into our mouths. If your interests are a little more active, you could make your menorah out of little clay baseball bats or hockey sticks. But if you're a little more active, you're probably not Jewish anyway.

YOU WILL NEED

2 pounds low-fire clay

Fettling knife (a butter knife will also work)

Wire tool (optional)

Underglazes in a variety of colors

Paintbrushes in a variety of sizes

Cone 06 clear glaze

נ Wedge clay and prepare a slab, ½ to 1 inch thick, using the knife as necessary.

ב Shape your menorah any way you like, using a wire tool if necessary. When you make your candle holes be sure to allow for clay shrinkage of about 20 percent.

ג When menorah is leather-hard, paint with underglazes. Bisque fire to cone 04.

ד Apply clear underglaze and fire to cone 06. When it's all done, kick back on the couch with a pile of latkes and bask in the glow of your creation.

EASY VARIATION You could also make your menorah from an oven-bake polymer clay like Fimo. Follow steps 1 and 2, using polymer clay instead of low-fire clay (you'll need about a pound). Bake according to package directions. When the menorah is cool, decorate with acrylic craft paint. Let the paint dry, then brush with a glossy clear acrylic sealer if you want a shiny finish. *Make sure* your clay, paint, and sealer are nonflammable.

You'll notice the candles have been lit in the wrong direction.
This is because they were lit in the Southern Hemisphere.

Mah-Jongg Menorah

We're not sure where our mah-jongg set came from. We never bought one; we were never given one; and yet we have one. We think they must just be standard issue for Jewish kids. Unfortunately, we never learned how to play. We tried and gave up. So we made a menorah out of the tiles instead, a project that proved to be much easier than the game itself. You can make one yourself in just a few minutes for very little gelt.

This project will require you to visit a hardware store, a place you've probably never been before. We know—it's scary. But this is one project you can't call your contractor for. So be brave and sally forth. You'll find the hardware store is a shop flowing with milk, honey, and all sorts of little findings the Jewish crafter can put to good use.

YOU WILL NEED

Good, nonflammable craft glue, such as Aleene's Tacky Glue

2 hex nuts, 1 inch in diameter

Metal bracket (we used a 9-inch stair bracket)

1 hex nut, ¾ inch in diameter

9 mah-jongg tiles

9 Keps nuts, size ⅜-16, or any nut that strikes your fancy (square nuts, cap nuts, and serrated nuts are all pretty snazzy)

א Glue your two 1-inch hex nuts to the bottom of your metal bracket. Allow to set.

ב Glue the ¾-inch hex nut to the bottom of a mah-jongg tile. Allow to set, then glue to the center of the metal bracket. Glue four mah-jongg tiles on either side for a total of nine.

ג Glue Keps nuts to the top of each tile. Allow to set.

ד All done! Keep it for yourself, or give it to Bubbe? Better make two.

Hanukkah Headband

One December we were out shopping and noticed everyone else was wearing a silly holiday headband. We saw reindeer antlers, holly, and Christmas tree branches. But where were the menorot? It didn't seem fair. Jews are always strapping things to their heads—yarmulkes, phylacteries, corrective eyewear—and there we were, bland and bareheaded. So we scurried home and whipped this up. It makes us feel as glamorous as a Las Vegas showgirl.

YOU WILL NEED

Scissors

⅛ yard blue felt

Straight pins

Narrow plastic headband

Sewing machine or needle and thread

⅛ yard white felt

1 pipe cleaner, cut to 8 inches long

8 pipe cleaners, cut to 6 inches long

⅛ yard yellow felt

א Cut two strips from blue felt, each 1 inch wide and 16 inches long. Pin together, wrong-sides facing. Sew along side edges as close to edge as possible, to form a tube. Use this tube to cover your headband. Cut off excess felt and stitch ends closed.

ב Cut two strips from white felt, each ¾ inch wide and 28 inches long. Pin together, wrong-sides facing. Sew along side edges as close to edge as possible, to form a tube. Cut this tube into eight 3-inch-long pieces and one 4-inch-long piece. These will form the candles.

ג Make a small snip, close to the seam, in the center of your blue felt headband. Make another small snip close to the seam on the opposite side. Thread your 8-inch-long pipe cleaner in one hole and out the other, making sure it goes under the plastic headband. This will be the wire form for the candle. Slip the 4-inch-long piece of white felt over the pipe cleaner.

ד Repeat Step 3 with the rest of the pipe cleaners and white felt sleeves, spacing candles 1¼ inch apart.

ה Cut nine flame shapes out of yellow felt and stitch one to the top of each candle. Voila! Your Hanukkah Headband is finished. Pop it on your noggin and go light up the night.

Latke Gravlax

These uptown potato pancakes pay tribute to nice Jewish boy Andy Kaufman and his alter egos, Latka Gravas and Las Vegas Lounge Legend Tony Clifton. You'll need to work fast as latke batter has a nasty tendency to turn black if allowed to stand too long. Of course, if you're planning a goth Hanukkah party, let it stand as long as you can.

YOU WILL NEED

2 pounds potatoes, peeled

1 large onion, quartered

2 tablespoons matzo meal or flour

2 eggs, separated

¼ cup fresh chives, finely chopped

2 teaspoons salt

½ teaspoon pepper

Oil for frying (about ½ cup)

6 ounces thinly sliced lox

¾ cup sour cream

3 ounces golden caviar (optional)

Preheat oven to 325°F. Place two baking sheets in oven to warm up.

In a food processor, shred potatoes and onion finely. Chefs lacking a food processor can grate by hand. Transfer potato-onion mixture to a colander lined with paper towels and press firmly to drain off excess liquid.

In a large bowl, combine potato-onion mixture, matzo meal or flour, egg yolks, 2 tablespoons chives, salt, and pepper. In a separate bowl beat egg whites until stiff but not dry. Fold egg whites into potato mixture.

Heat oil in a heavy frying pan. When oil is hot, drop tablespoons of batter into the pan, spreading each drop into a 3-inch pancake. Cook pancakes 3 to 4 minutes on each side. Transfer pancakes to baking sheets and place in oven to keep warm. Repeat until batter is used up.

To serve, garnish pancakes with lox, 2 tablespoons of chives, dollops of sour cream, and caviar, if desired. Offer to guests in your best Latka Gravas voice: *iddy biddy ba?* When there's only one pancake left, instruct guests to wrestle for it.

SERVES 6

EASY, SLEAZY VARIATION It must be admitted that making latkes is not always as fast and fun as everyone pretends it is. We enjoy eating them, but setting off the smoke detector, getting potato shreds all over the kitchen floor, stinking like fried potato for days—we can live without all of that. If you can, too, just mix up a batch of instant mashed potatoes, form into patties, and panfry in lots of oil. Then skip the lox and caviar and douse these bad boys in ranch.

Las Veggies Menorah Salad

Our favorite aspect of Jewish cooking, like our favorite aspect of Las Vegas, is the artifice. Nothing is served in its natural form. We mold salads in the shape of religious symbols, bake cakes in the form of the Torah, and sculpt ice into busts of Bar Mitzvah boys. A friend tells us about one Bat Mitzvah she attended, which featured a performance by the Solid Gold Dancers and ice sculptures of the Bat Mitzvah girl in dance poses. This classic recipe, for a menorah made from asparagus, isn't exactly a Vegas revue, but it's sure to light up your lunch.

YOU WILL NEED

28 asparagus spears

27 toybox tomatoes (use cherry tomatoes if you can't find the smaller toybox variety)

⅓ cup salad oil

1 tablespoon wine vinegar

2 teaspoons Dijon mustard

3 hard-boiled eggs (optional)

א Steam asparagus until tender. Jews traditionally cook vegetables until they're the texture of pudding, but you can make them as al dente as you like. Allow asparagus to cool.

ב Cut asparagus in thirds and tomatoes in half.

ג For the next part, you'll need six salad plates. On each salad plate, arrange nine asparagus thirds to look like menorah candles. Top each candle with a tomato half, to resemble a flame. Use another five asparagus thirds to make the base of the menorah.

ד In a small bowl, mix together salad oil, wine vinegar, and mustard to make a dressing.

ה Drizzle dressing over menorah salads. If you like, you can garnish them by grating hard-boiled egg over the top. Chill until ready to serve.

SERVES 6

It's much tastier than a 99¢ shrimp cocktail, and Kosher, too!

**Get Lit Wine Bottle Lamp,
page 94**

PART 6

PURIM

bottoms up

Purim is big on Bar, low on Mitzvah. It's the campiest of all Jewish holidays, and hence, our favorite. You wear costumes. You drink too much. Your friends bring you baked goods. What's not to love?

Well, the hangover, but we won't worry about that now. Purim is the day rules don't apply. It's the only day of the year Orthodox Jews are allowed to cross-dress. After seeing your rabbi in a leather skirt and fishnets, who wouldn't need a drink? So dress up, drink up, and party down.

On Purim we party like rock stars, and that means eating ourselves sick. Tradition dictates we host a Purim Seudah, or feast, in the afternoon. Our favorite theme is a Monsters of Rock Backstage Buffet. Call yourselves Mötley Jüe and make your roadies serve green M&M's and Cristal. Enjoy a slice of Better than Neil Diamond Cake (see page 98) and Jammin' Taschen (see page 97) while you bask in the post-show glow of the Get Lit Wine Bottle Lamp (see page 94). Distribute Top Shelf Shalach Manot (see page 95) to your groupies. *L'Chaim!*

Get Lit Wine Bottle Lamp

Man, oh Manischewitz. It's the drink of choice for rabbis, winos, and eight-year-old girls. Responsible for every Jew's first buzz, it retains a special place in our hearts even after we learn to appreciate drier wines. An empty Manischewitz wine bottle becomes a fun, funky lamp that will keep you lit long after the wine is gone. Of course, you'll have to drink the wine first. If you can't stand it straight, take it from us: it makes a surprisingly good sangria.

YOU WILL NEED

Empty Manischewitz bottle, clean and dry, with label intact

Assorted decorations: rhinestones, beads, Star of David pendants, fringe, or whatever you like

Good nonflammable craft glue, such as Aleene's Tacky Glue

Lamp oil

Fitting to convert a bottle to an oil-burning lamp (Widely available at hardware stores, candle shops, even head shops. Look for a product like Winelights.)

א This project is so easy you could almost do it drunk. Just glue your decorations to your bottle and allow to set.

ב Fill bottle with lamp oil and install fitting, according to package instructions.

ג Light wick and bask in the glow of success.

Top Shelf Shalach Manot

It's traditional to give *shalach manot,* baskets of goodies, to friends on Purim. Some people serve up a tangerine and two Oreos on a paper plate. Not you, rock star. You really put on a show. Well, at the very least, you decorate the paper plate, and you never give out less than *three* Oreos. But if you want to raise the bar without breaking your back, try these ideas for extra-special shalach manot. Here's a "Friendly Skies Snack Sack," for your high-flying friends.

YOU WILL NEED

Pretty paper sack (If you happen to have an air sickness bag, use that. Trust us, it's funny.)

Lining paper (look for tissue paper printed with clouds or planes)

Shot-sized bottles of booze

Packets of peanuts, pretzels, or if you're ritzy, cashews or macadamia nuts

Sugar cookies shaped like airplanes

Travel trinkets: little plastic wings, tiny model airplanes, or whatever you think your friends might enjoy

א Line your bag with paper, then fill with goodies.

ב Present your fabulous creations to your flabbergasted friends. Be gracious when they hand you a paper plate with a tangerine and two Oreos in return.

VARIATION ONE "The Happy Hippy Hemp Sack," for the nice and natural crowd. Use a hemp bag or basket, and line with tissue paper with a tie-dye or psychedelic print. Fill with: bottle of organic wine, granola bars, gorp, incense, beeswax candles.

VARIATION TWO "The Trash Bag," for your junk food–loving friends. Use a plain brown paper bag, and line with a few pages from a tabloid. Fill with: bottle of malt liquor, an assortment of packaged snack cakes, an assortment of junky candies, little bags of chips, professional wrestling figurines (Goldberg would be best).

We hope you like jammin', too.

Jammin' Taschen

We don't quite understand the Jewish affection for reggae music. It seems odd that a people as neurotic as we would enjoy music as mellow as that, but it's true. Our field experience indicates reggae is the only music Jewish men listen to between the ages of sixteen and twenty-five. And perhaps they should. We have a lot in common with our Rasta reggae brothers. We both yearn for Zion and prefer warm climates. Jews have been in Jamaica for more than 500 years, and a Jewish family is responsible for our second-favorite Jamaican export: Myer's Rum.

Purim seems like the perfect time to pay tribute to the music we love so much with a batch of these tasty pastries. Also known as Peter Toshen and Hey Mohn Taschen, they're sure to have you feelin' Irie.

YOU WILL NEED

⅔ cup margarine or butter

½ cup sugar

1 egg

½ teaspoon vanilla

½ teaspoon lemon rind (optional)

3 cups flour, plus more for rolling

1 teaspoon baking powder

2 cups filling (use strawberry jam, lemon curd, and jalapeño jelly for a red-yellow-and-green Jamaican flag effect, or use canned poppyseed *mohn* filling)

א Cream together the margarine or butter and sugar in a large bowl. Add the egg, vanilla, and lemon rind, if using. Add the dry ingredients and sing "Stir It Up" until mixed well. Separate dough into four balls and refrigerate for an hour or so.

ב Preheat oven to 375°F. Grease cookie sheets.

ג On a floured surface, roll out each ball of dough to ⅛-inch thickness. Cut out circles using a cup with a 2½-inch diameter.

ד Place a scant tablespoon of filling in the center of each circle. Fold three sides of each circle over to form a triangle. Pinch edges to seal. Place triangles on cookie sheets and bake 10 to 15 minutes, or until golden.

MAKES APPROXIMATELY 3 DOZEN

Better than Neil Diamond Cake

Is there anything kitschier than "Better than . . ." cakes? Better than Robert Redford, Better than Brad Pitt, Better than Sex . . . the names may change, but the ingredients remain the same. Chocolate cake mix, sweetened condensed milk, and whipped topping make sweet, sweet love. Here's the Jewish version, named in honor of rock and roll sex symbol Neil Diamond. We've topped it with halvah instead of the usual Heath Bars because halvah is more Hebrew—and more happening. Serve this with some Red Red Wine and you'll have a Holly Holy holiday.

YOU WILL NEED

18.25-ounce box chocolate
  cake mix

14-ounce can sweetened
  condensed milk

2 cups hot fudge topping

12-ounce container frozen
  whipped topping, thawed

Five 1-ounce bars halvah,
  finely chopped

א Bake cake according to package directions in a 9-by-13-inch glass pan.

ב While cake is still warm, poke holes in top with the end of a wooden spoon. Pour sweetened condensed milk over the top. Refrigerate for 4 hours.

ג Microwave hot fudge topping until soft. Pour over cake. Allow to set. Spread whipped topping over cake and garnish with chopped halvah.

SERVES 12

It's sweeter than Caroline.

PART 7

PASSOVER
let my people go

Among the Jewish holidays, Passover is the Freedom Jam. But it doesn't always feel that way. Anyone who's ever kashered a kitchen for Passover knows that Obsessive Compulsive Disorder is endemically Jewish. Passover's in the details, but don't let the details gang up on you. Remember the freedom. Remember the fun.

There's big fun to be had. Passover is the only holiday that actually revolves around a dinner party. The Passover story is so rich, it lends itself to any number of themes. You could, for instance, host a "Darth Seder" as a tribute to *Star Wars*. We can't help thinking the plot was borrowed from Exodus. Luke is Moses. Princess Leia is Miriam. She's also a *princess,* for goodness' sake. And check out that pharaoh head on Darth. *Dayenu.*

Host a super-classy opera-themed "Die Sedermaus," and make all the participants sing their parts. Or take the low road and throw a "Crassover" seder, featuring junk food and tasteless jokes. Crazy college kids can make the most of the season with a "Spring Break Seder." Respond to every

Passover Purse,
page 103

haggadah passage with a "woo hoo!" Serve blender drinks with suggestive names and the morning after will become known as "Passhangover." Next Year in Daytona Beach! We've been to a high-camp "Gayder," a fabulous event marred only by a catfight over the Four Questions, when it was announced they would be read not by the youngest, but by the youngest looking. A struggle for the seat with the most flattering lighting ensued. And we have some friends who keep threatening to host a chips-dips-chains-and-whips seder as a tribute to our, ahem, escape from bondage.

But the theme we like best is "Seder at the Children's Table." Children get to do all the really cool stuff at the seder: ask the Four Questions, hunt for the afikoman, whine, say inappropriate things with impunity, and fall asleep at the table. Re-create happy memories of misbehaving while your parents were away at the grown-ups' table with this party theme. Turn the hagaddah reading into a game, with a Magic Word of the Day, like "rabbi" or "Egypt" or "pharaoh," that prompts guests to answer goofy questions, don costumes, or read in pig latin. If things get dull, interrupt the proceedings with an impromptu round of "Exodus Tag." Serve kid-friendly foods like Matzo Meteors (see page 109), Little Miss Muffins (see page 110), and Mud Pie (see page 111). Present the goods on the Schoolbook Seder Plate (see page 105) and the Gefilte Fish Platter (see page 106). And if you get tired, just send yourself to your room.

Passover Purse

This is an ambitious project, most suitable for shut-ins and obsessive-compulsives. It will take you at least a hundred hours, and you'll need more than 20,000 beads. But you will end up with a one-of-a-kind piece of heirloom kitsch. Some future Passover, you can pass it down to your grandchild. The purse may even be the reason you have future grandchildren. Every time we carry it, we get marriage proposals. Go figure.

YOU WILL NEED

Box of Manischewitz matzo meal, clean, empty, and intact

Scissors

Roll of medical tape

Green and orange markers

Cardboard

¼ yard fun fur

Good craft glue, such as Aleene's Tacky Glue

1 snap

10,500 size 11 seed beads in orange (2 to 3 hanks)

6,000 size 11 seed beads in green (1 to 2 hanks)

4,500 size 11 seed beads in opaque white (1 hank)

250 size 11 seed beads in yellow (or smaller, if you can find them—size 15 is ideal)

200 size 11 seed beads in gold

Foam brush

Glossy clear acrylic sealer

Toothpick

13 large plastic beads

12-inch pipe cleaner

Duct tape

2 inches of green ribbon

Green and orange felt

Cut the sides and front of the top but leave boxtop attached at the back, so it opens like a hinged box. Stick a strip of medical tape along the outside and the inside where the boxtop is still attached to the rest of the box, so the cardboard won't wear out and rip if you flex this joint a lot. Color the medical tape on the outside with a green marker.

Cut cardboard pieces the same size as the front, back, and sides. Glue fun fur to these pieces, then glue cardboard to inside of box, to fortify. Seal any raw cardboard edges with medical tape. Color the tape with orange or green marker so it blends. Glue the male half of a snap to the front, dead center just above the white oval that contains the Manischewitz logo (you'll use the snap to make a clasp later).

Glue your 20,000-plus beads to the top and sides of the box, using the box design as a template. Be sure to leave two pea-sized areas clear on the boxtop, about half an inch in, so you can put on a handle later.

When the glue is set, use the foam brush to coat the beads with glossy clear acrylic sealer. Allow to dry, then apply another coat. When that's dry, using the toothpick, puncture two small holes in the top in the pea-sized spaces you've left clear of beads. Center the thirteen large plastic beads on the pipe cleaner. Push the ends of pipe cleaner through the holes you just made in the top. Secure the ends of pipe cleaner to the inside of the top with duct tape. Next, make your clasp. Glue or stitch the female half of your snap to the back of your 2-inch length of heavy ribbon. Center ribbon and secure with duct tape to the inside of the box top. Glue green felt to the inside of the boxtop, and orange felt to the bottom of the box.

A is for an awesome seder plate.

Schoolbook Seder Plate

There's no reason a seder plate has to be stiff and stodgy. And there's no reason it can't learn the young 'uns a thing or two—that's what Passover's all about. Why is this seder plate different from all other seder plates? Because it's stylin' and stylized with nifty '50s cartoon drawings reminiscent of Dick and Jane, or, in this case, David and Rachel. See David and Rachel have the coolest Passover ever.

YOU WILL NEED

3 pounds low-fire clay

Fettling knife (a butter knife will also work)

Paintbrushes in a variety of sizes

Underglazes in a variety of colors

Clear cone 06 glaze

Wedge the clay and prepare a ¾-inch-thick slab, using the knife as necessary. Cut out a circle about 15 inches in diameter. You may want to use a store-bought platter as a template. Add a foot on the underside of the plate.

Allow clay to dry completely. Then go to town on your seder plate with your paintbrushes and underglazes, making sure to include spaces for the zeroah (shank bone), haroset, lettuce, karpas (green veggies), maror (bitter herbs), and egg. Add a cute little cartoon scene in the middle of the plate. Here, David and Rachel enjoy a traditional Passover seder.

Bisque fire to cone 04.

Apply a clear glaze and fire to cone 06.

EASY VARIATION If you don't happen to have a kiln in your basement (and if you're Jewish, you probably don't), this is a great project to do at a paint-your-own pottery joint. You could also just paint a store-bought platter at home, but if you do, *make sure* your paint is approved for contact with food. If it doesn't say it's food-safe on the label, it probably isn't. If you can't find food-safe products, just use your plate for decorative purposes.

Gefilte Fish Platter

According to recent findings, Jewish food has been around much longer than originally thought. This Passover platter depicts a specimen of the ancient and exceedingly rare gefilte fish, found only in the lakes of the Catskill region. We understand it's related to the Plastic Sturgeon, but you'd have to ask a shtickthyologist to be sure.

YOU WILL NEED

3 pounds low-fire clay

Fettling knife (a butter knife will also work)

Underglazes in a variety of colors

Paintbrushes in a variety of sizes

Clear cone 06 glaze

Wedge the clay and prepare a ¾-inch-thick slab, using the knife as necessary. Cut out an oval about 12 by 6 inches.

Attach a foot to the bottom of the oval. Make it about 1 inch tall so it can be mounted on the wall, as well as served on a table.

Once platter is completely dry, paint it with whatever you imagine a gefilte fish to look like in the wild. You may want to consult scientific illustrations of fish for inspiration. Add imaginary Latin text to make it look official. Here we see the *Piscis Piscis Gefiltavus*.

Bisque fire to cone 04.

Apply a clear glaze and fire to cone 06.

EASY VARIATION If you don't happen to have a kiln in your basement (and if you're Jewish, you probably don't), this is a great project to do at a paint-your-own pottery joint. You could also just paint a store-bought platter at home, but if you do, *make sure* your paint is approved for contact with food. If it doesn't say it's food-safe on the label, it probably isn't. If you can't find food-safe products, just use your platter for decorative purposes.

PISCIS PISCIS GEFILTAVUS
(Gefilte Fish)

found in the Lakes of the Catskill region

The female of the species sports slingbacks and a matching handbag.

It's the soup that
eats like five meals.

Matzo Meteors

Forget Reform vs. Orthodox, Labor vs. Likud, Dove vs. Hawk. The issue that really divides the Jewish people is Floaters vs. Sinkers. We happen to be Sinker people. We think Floater people are nuts. Sinkers! This is our recipe for the ultimate Sinker: the Matzo Meteor. What a meteor does to a space ship, this matzo ball will do to your gastrointestinal tract. But it hurts so good.

YOU WILL NEED

8 eggs

2 teaspoons salt

Dash pepper

1 cup water

⅔ cup oil

3⅓ cups matzo meal

4 quarts soup or water

א In a medium bowl, beat eggs lightly with a fork. Add salt, pepper, water, and oil. Mix in matzo meal and stir until blended. Refrigerate for 15 minutes.

ב Roll batter into walnut-sized balls and toss into 4 quarts of boiling soup or water. Cook for 30 minutes. Strain.

SERVES 12

Little Miss Muffins

Forget curds and whey. Also known as Queen of Denial Matzo Rolls, these delicious little popovers help us get through a week without bread. And if you're hosting a Darth Seder, they may be used to simulate Princess Leia's idiosyncratic hairdo.

YOU WILL NEED

2 cups water

1 cup vegetable oil

2 teaspoons salt

2 cups matzo meal

8 eggs, lightly beaten

א Preheat oven to 450°F and lightly grease two muffin tins.

ב In a large saucepan, bring water, oil, and salt to a boil. Remove from heat. Stir in matzo meal and eggs. Mix well.

ג Refrigerate mixture for 20 minutes.

ד Plop batter into muffin tins and bake 20 minutes. Allow to cool.

MAKES 24 MUFFINS

Mud Pie

It just about killed us every year when the Girl Scout cookies arrived smack in the middle of Passover. All our classmates were enjoying Peanut Butter Tagalongs and Thin Mints, and we were stuck with sad, gummy macaroons. We would have felt a lot better if we'd had this decadent chocolate torte. Here's mud in your eye!

YOU WILL NEED

1 cup margarine (use butter if the meal is milchig)

2 cups sugar

8 eggs

12 ounces semisweet chocolate chips

2 cups almonds, cashews, or hazelnuts, ground to the texture of cornmeal

⅔ cup matzo cake meal

½ cup jam or preserves (Raspberry, apricot, and orange marmalade are particularly good. Grape is particularly gross.)

Cocoa for dusting (optional)

א Preheat oven to 375°F. Grease bottoms of two 9-inch cake pans.

ב In a large bowl, combine margarine and sugar. Beat until fluffy, then mix in eggs.

ג Melt chocolate in a double boiler. Allow to cool for a minute, then add to the margarine-sugar-egg mixture. Stir in nuts and matzo meal and mix well.

ד Pour mixture into cake pans. Bake 25 to 30 minutes.

ה When cakes have cooled, turn out and spread jam on one and top with the other layer.

ו If you like, dust cake with cocoa.

SERVES 12

Today, I am a bookend.
(Page 114)

SHAVUOT
PART 8
milking it

Shavuot is the shady lady of the Jewish calendar. No non-Jews have heard of it, and few Jews observe it in any way. Which is a shame, because it's got some of the best customs, like eating all the dairy we can stand. We're not sure why it's traditional to celebrate the giving of the Torah by raising our cholesterol levels, but we're happy it is.

Among the Jewish holidays, Shavuot is the all-night party. We stay up and study Torah, but there's plenty of time for snacking, too. And while stale Danish, gray scrambled eggs, and spiked punch were good enough for your Grad Night, you might want to try something a little more special for Shavuot. We recommend the Super Dairy Experience (see page 115) and a Shavuot Sugar Rush Buffet, stocked with enough cookies and caffeine to keep you going all night. The pièce de résistance: the Mount Sinai Sundae (see page 116). Use the Bar Mitzvah Bokher Bookends (see page 114) as a centerpiece.

Bar Mitzvah Bokher Bookends

Shavuot is the scholar's holiday. Why not give your favorite scholars these beautiful bookends to keep their tomes organized? The Bar/Bat Mitzvah figurines will remind them that study is rewarded with savings bonds, fountain pens, and tasteful gold jewelry.

YOU WILL NEED

Foam brush

4 books of slightly different sizes (Pick books you never plan on reading, since you'll be coating them with paint and glue.)

Plain metal bookends

Two 2-by-2-inch cubes to use as a platform (cardboard, styrofoam, and wood are all fine)

Gold acrylic craft paint

2 Bar/Bat Mitzvah cake toppers (available at cake decorating stores)

Good craft glue, such as Aleene's Tacky Glue

א Using the foam brush, coat books, bookends, and 2-by-2-inch cubes in gold paint. Allow to dry. Add more coats until everything is good and shiny, allowing paint to dry between coats.

ב Glue cake toppers to 2-by-2-inch cubes. Allow to set.

ג Glue two books together, with the smaller book in front, then glue these books to a bookend. Then glue a cake topper-and-platform unit to the front. Repeat with the other books, bookend, and cake topper unit.

ד Step back and study your crafty kitsch wizardry. You're pretty smart yourself.

The Super Dairy Experience

Have you ever been experienced? This savory love child of macaroni and cheese and noodle kugel will blow your mind. Well, it'll blow *something*. We don't think it's possible for a food to contain more saturated fat. Excuse me while I kiss the sky.

YOU WILL NEED

3 sticks plus 4 tablespoons margarine or butter

4 cups breadcrumbs (we recommend you make them yourself from stale challah or bagels)

2 pounds elbow macaroni or egg noodles

6 cups grated cheddar cheese, or a mixture of cheddar, Swiss, and Monterey Jack

16 ounces cream cheese, cubed

4 cups half-and-half

4 eggs, lightly beaten

½ teaspoon salt

½ teaspoon white pepper

א Preheat oven to 350°F. Butter two 9-by-13 baking dishes.

ב Melt 1 stick plus 4 tablespoons margarine or butter, then combine with breadcrumbs in a small bowl. Set aside.

ג Bring a large pot of water to a boil. Add macaroni or noodles and cook just until tender. Drain and return to pot.

ד Melt 2 sticks of butter and pour over macaroni or noodles. Stir in grated cheese, cream cheese, half-and-half, eggs, salt, and pepper. Mix until cream cheese is melted.

ה Transfer mixture to baking dish or dishes and top with buttered breadcrumbs. Bake until golden brown and bubbly, about 35 minutes.

SERVES 12

Mount Sinai Sundae

Milk and honey are fine, but there's nothing wrong with hot fudge, either. On Shavuot we celebrate the giving of the Torah with a delicious re-creation of the site where it all went down.

YOU WILL NEED

Half gallon ice cream, softened (Use any flavor you like, but try to pick something somewhat realistic, color-wise. Coffee, chocolate, vanilla, and even mint chip are reasonable choices. Rainbow sherbet is not.)

2 cups hot fudge topping

¾ cup chopped almonds

2 cups whipped cream or whipped topping

א Dump ice cream on your serving platter. With a spatula, sculpt it into a mountain shape.

ב Microwave the hot fudge topping a few seconds, so it's spreadable but not so hot that it will liquefy the ice cream.

ג Spread hot fudge topping onto your ice cream mountain. Try to be artistic about it. Sprinkle chopped almonds on top to look like loose mountain dirt.

ד Dot on some whipped-cream cloud formations, then place your creation in the freezer until you're ready to serve.

SERVES 8

Scale this!

HEBONICS *(a glossary)*

Afikoman: piece of matzo ransomed for a reward on Passover

Ayzeh yofi: how cute/great/pretty

Balebusta: homemaker

Besamim: spices used in the Havdalah ceremony

Birkat Hamazon: grace after meals

Bokher: boy

B'tayavon: bon appetit

Bubbe: grandmother

Chavurah: a Jewish community

Dayenu: a song sung on Passover. Literally, "it would have sufficed us"

Drosh: sermon

Erev: eve

Fleishig: containing meat ingredients

Fresser: enthusiastic eater

Halachah: Jewish law

Haroset: a paste of fruit, wine, and nuts, meant to resemble the mortar Jewish slaves used. Served at Passover

Havdalah: a ceremony marking the end of Shabbat

Kasher: to render kosher

Kiddush: a prayer sanctifying Shabbat and holidays, recited over wine

Klaf: scroll inside a mezuzah

Kvell: gloat

Kvetch: complain

L'Chaim: to life! The Jewish "Cheers"

L'Shana Tova: Happy New Year

Machberet: notebook

Mensch: a good man

Mezuzah (plural *mezuzot*): A scroll inscribed with a prayer, affixed to the doorpost in Jewish homes. "Mezuzah" commonly refers to the case that holds the scroll

Milchig: containing dairy ingredients

Mishpocheh: family

Mitzvah (plural *mitzvot*): good deed, commandment

Mizrach: a plaque or wall hanging marking the eastern wall of the home

Naches: pride

Nosh (plural *nosherei*): snack

Pareve: without any meat or dairy products

Payess: sidelocks

Punim: face

Pushke: charity box

Rebbe: rabbi

Schmatte: rag. Slang for clothing

Seudah: festive meal

Shabbat / Shabbos: the Sabbath

Shalach Manot: baskets of goodies distributed on Purim

Shande: a shame

Shayna: pretty

Shofar: ram's horn, blown on Rosh Hashanah

Shul: synagogue

Siddur: prayerbook

Sukkah: a backyard hut we eat and sleep in on the holiday of Sukkot

Tallis: prayer shawl

Tchotchke: knickknack

Treyf: unkosher

Tzedakah: charity

Yahrzeit: memorial

Yarmulke: skullcap

Yom Tov: holiday

Zayde: grandfather

RESOURCES

No matter where you live, good Jewish kitsch can be yours. We grew up in a California cow town with the tiniest handful of Jews. But our lives were rich in Judaikitsch, so we know: you can find it or make it, wherever you may be. And if you're in what seems to be a tchotchke-free galaxy, take heart. The best finds often come from unexpected places. We found so much good material in purportedly Catholic Maryland that by the end of our trip, we were calling it Murrayland. Here are some ideas to get you started.

jewish bookstores and synagogue gift shops

Your first stop. The only problem with these, we find, is that the stock tends to be a little too tasteful. Go for the low-end items and tacky them up.

cake decorating and party supply stores

Look in the Bar Mitzvah section and the Hanukkah section for unusual accessories. These stores are also great for paper goods and materials that aren't strictly Jewish, like Hawaiian decorations for your Sukkot luau.

craft stores

Loaded with nondenominational supplies of all kinds.

web resources

1800dreidel.com: A fabulous selection of Jewish fabrics and craft supplies.

Archiemcphee.com: A small assortment of Jewish kitsch you won't find anywhere else, and a large selection of non-Jewish kitsch that will blow your mind.

eBay.com: We hate to mention it, because we're afraid you'll outbid us on our faves, but it's a good resource for both Judaica and Judaikitsch, especially if you live in an area without any Jewish stores.

Jewish.com: A large selection of Judaica that's more tasteful than tacky, but you can always kitsch your purchases up yourself.

Paperjudaica.com: The biggest assortment of Jewish party supplies online.

FURTHER READING

kitsch

Dorfles, Gillo, et al. *Kitsch: The World of Bad Taste.* New York: Universe Books, 1970.

Friedländer, Saul. *Reflections of Nazism: An Essay on Kitsch and Death.* Translated by Thomas Weyr. New York: Harper & Row, 1984.

Moles, Abraham A. *Le Kitsch: l'art du bonheur.* Paris: Maison Mame, 1971.

Olalquiaga, Celeste. *The Artificial Kingdom: A Treasury of the Kitsch Experience.* New York: Parthenon Books, 1998.

jewish domestic history

Heinze, Andrew R. *Adapting to Abundance: Jewish Immigrants, Mass Consumption, and the Search for American Identity.* New York: Columbia University Press, 1990.

Joselit, Jenna Weissman. *The Wonders of America: Reinventing Jewish Culture, 1880–1950.* New York: Hill and Wang, 1994.

jewish practice

Greenberg, Blu. *How to Run a Traditional Jewish Household.* New York: Simon & Schuster, 1983.

Strassfeld, Michael, et al. *The Jewish Catalog: A Do-It-Yourself Kit.* Philadelphia: Jewish Publication Society of America, 1973.

Waskow, Arthur I. *Seasons of Our Joy: A Modern Guide to the Jewish Holidays.* New York: Beacon Press, 1990.

jewish cooking

Blau, Esther, et al. *Spice and Spirit: The Complete Kosher Jewish Cookbook.* New York: Lubavitch Women's Organization, 1997.

Nathan, Joan. *The Jewish Holiday Kitchen.* New York: Schocken Books, 1998.

jewish craft

Tupa, Mae Rockland. *The New Work of Our Hands: Contemporary Jewish Needlework and Quilts.* Radnor, Pennsylvania: Chilton Book Company, 1994.

Zoloth, Joan. *Jewish Holiday Treats: Recipes and Crafts for the Whole Family.* San Francisco: Chronicle Books, 2000.

acknowledgments This book was very much a family affair, and we're indebted to the whole mishpocheh. Thanks, first, to our parents, whose help was instrumental; what projects they didn't directly contribute, their sensibilities inspired. We're grateful to Peter McGrath, Dan McGrath, Wendy McGrath, Maureen Neff, Tim Neff, Miriam Schleicher, and Mitzi Schleicher for putting us up and putting up with us. Thanks to Courtney Vaughn and David Olem for their culinary expertise; to Colleen Flanigan, Angela Hernandez, and Daniel Archer for their patience; and to Ryan Gray, who ate the cat food. Finally, we thank our editor Mikyla Bruder, assistant editor Jodi Davis, designer Benjamin Shaykin, and photographer Dwight Eschliman. Their respective and collective brilliance made this megillah and we're much obliged to them and the whole Chronicle family.

PATTERNS

Pet Yarmulke (for cats)

Pet Yarmulke (for dogs)

The "Steppin' Out" Yarmulke

TABLE OF EQUIVALENTS

The exact equivalents in the following tables have been rounded for convenience.

liquid and dry measures

U.S.	METRIC
¼ teaspoon	1.25 milliliters
½ teaspoon	2.5 milliliters
1 teaspoon	5 milliliters
1 tablespoon (3 teaspoons)	15 milliliters
1 fluid ounce (2 tablespoons)	30 milliliters
¼ cup	65 milliliters
⅓ cup	80 milliliters
1 cup	235 milliliters
1 pint (2 cups)	480 milliliters
1 quart (4 cups, 32 ounces)	950 milliliters
1 gallon (4 quarts)	3.8 liters
1 ounce (by weight)	28 grams
1 pound	454 grams
2.2 pounds	1 kilogram

length measures

U.S.	METRIC
⅛ inch	3 millimeters
¼ inch	6 millimeters
½ inch	12 millimeters
1 inch	2.5 centimeters

oven temperatures

FAHRENHEIT	CELSIUS	GAS
250	120	½
275	140	1
300	150	2
325	160	3
350	180	4
375	190	5
400	200	6
425	220	7
450	230	8
475	240	9
500	260	10

Hanukkah Headband (page 88)